# THE
# WINE LOVER'S
## —GUIDE TO—
## *Burgundy*

# THE WINE LOVER'S
## —GUIDE TO—
# *Burgundy*

—MICHAEL BUSSELLE—

PAVILION
MICHAEL JOSEPH

First published in Great Britain in 1990 by
PAVILION BOOKS LIMITED
196 Shaftesbury Avenue, London WC2H 8JL
in association with Michael Joseph Limited
27 Wrights Lane, Kensington, London W8 5TZ

Photographs and wine tours text
copyright © Michael Busselle 1986
Wine-buying guides compiled by Graham Chidgey &
Lorne Mackillop copyright © Pavilion Books 1986
Other text by Ned Halley copyright © Pavilion Books 1990

Series Editor Ned Halley
Designed by Bridgewater Design Ltd
Map by Lorraine Harrison

A CIP catalogue record for this book is available from the
British Library

ISBN 1-85145-2427

10  9  8  7  6  5  4  3  2  1

Printed and bound in Spain by Graficas Estella S.A.

*Previous pages: A château in the hills of Northern Beaujolais*

# Contents

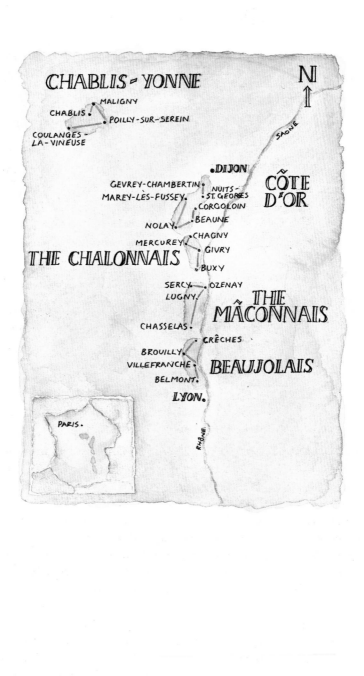

# Introduction

*The famous walled vineyard and château of Clos de Vougeot*

ROM CHABLIS, its northern outpost, to the far-distant reaches of the Beaujolais in the warm south, Burgundy encompasses a wide world of wine. The great vineyards at the region's heart, with proud names like Chevalier Montrachet and Domaine de la Romanée Conti, inspire nothing short of reverence among connoisseurs. But Burgundy has other, more approachable wines that are a delight to discover along the region's hundreds of miles of idyllic Routes des Vins.

Unlike most other winemaking regions of France, there are few individual estates planted around a central house at which the wine is made by the owner. Most of the vineyards belonged to the Church before the French Revolution, were sold off to a large collection of buyers – and have since been passed on from generation to generation, being divided up into smaller and smaller parcels of land.

A good example is the famous walled vineyard of Clos de Vougeot, in which a huge Cistercian monastery stands. Since the Church was stripped of this treasured possession two centuries ago, the vineyard – covering 125 acres – has been divided up into no less than 85 individually owned parts. The monastery now serves a distinctly secular purpose – as the hall of pomp and ceremony for the local winemakers' association.

The consequence for the vineyard visitor is that the convenient, interesting tour of vines, winery, cellars and château that might be possible all on one site in, say, Bordeaux is very much less easy to arrange in

Burgundy. While grapes might go briefly to local press-houses at vintage time, most of the newly made wine is soon moved to the great cellars of the *négociants-éléveurs* in Beaune and Nuits St Georges. These are dealers who buy wines from the growers, then *élévent* ('raise') them in their own properties.

The great cellars of famous firms like Paul Drouhin, Patriarche Père & Fils and Reine Pédauque can be visited in Beaune. Each firm has a vast array of wines to taste – and to buy. The range will start with simple

*An orderly vineyard dense with the green foliage of early summer near
the Mâconnais wine village of Azé*

Bourgogne *appellation contrôlée* at 30FF or so a bottle, with prices climbing steeply to the astronomical levels for which burgundy is deservedly notorious.

Tempting though it always is to buy wines *in situ*, do beware the very highly priced burgundies – they may well be significantly cheaper at home.

*Ripened Gamay grapes await the pickers on the steep stony slopes of a
Beaujolais vineyard*

Exchange rates may determine this to some extent, but more important is
the fact that French wine firms and merchants tend to place even higher
retail mark-ups on their top wines than do retailers in, say, the UK or the
USA. This applies particularly to mature wines which the merchant has
held in stock for quite a number of years. You are likely to find prices for
such wines have inflated more rapidly in France than they have at home.

None of this is to say that it is anything other than a delight to browse in
the wine shops that proliferate in Burgundy's towns – Beaune in particular.
If you are in search of good Côte d'Or wines, consider those from the more
modest end of the price range. The village wines of Aloxe-Corton – simply
labelled Aloxe-Corton – can be quite sensational reds, for example, and
priced around 90FF compared to 150-200FF for a *Grand Cru* Corton of the
same vintage. There is, of course, a difference in quality, but the Aloxe still
lets you discover the character of Corton – and appreciating the fine
variations between the 'good' and the 'great' wines tends to be a
psychological exercise as much as a gustatory one!

One thing about which you should harbour no illusions is the importance
of vintages. Burgundy is the most northerly of all winemaking regions in
which it is possible to make decent red wine, and its weather is treacherous.
Some vintages are badly affected by frost, by torrential downpours or simply
by lack of sufficient sunlight to ripen the grapes.

As a very general guide, recent vintages compare for quality as follows:
1988 was excellent for reds, good for whites; 1987 was mixed but some reds

*Harvesting the grapes on the slopes above the village of Chiroubles in the Beaujolais*

and fewer whites were very good indeed; 1986 produced good reds and some of the best whites in living memory; 1985 was precisely the reverse of 1986 for whites and reds; 1984 was dismal for everything; 1983 ranged from poor to excellent for reds and whites alike – a tricky and very expensive vintage to buy now; 1982 was mixed too, without reaching 1983's heights, but the wines are now cheaper, more ready to drink and quite delicious on the whole.

All the foregoing applies mainly to the wines of the Côte d'Or. In the less vaunted districts of the Auxerrois (next to Chablis) and the Beaujolais, Chalonnais and Mâconnais, the wines tend to be drunk younger – and they can, happily, be bought at prices that make shopping for them a rather less heart-searching business.

In these regions, there are many co-operatives selling wine direct to the public at bargain prices. Many small estates, too, offer *vente directe* (direct sale) and *caveaux de dégustation* (tasting cellars) to tempt passing motorists on the well-worn Routes des Vins that wind from one village to the next.

Here you can expect an enthusiastic welcome, for growers in, say, Mercurey or the villages of Mâcon are all too aware of the lure of their grandiloquently named neighbours to the north and are anxious that their own wines should have some small share of the limelight. And rightly so, for the wines of Burgundy's *outré* regions often have as much charm as the aristocratic *grands vins* from just across that unseen and sometimes incomprehensible line drawn under the rules of *appellation d'origine contrôlée*.

# A Tour of Chablis and the Yonne

*Above: Gently contoured hillsides, like this freshly ploughed
wheatfield, are typical of the Yonne countryside near Chablis
Left: A shady lane threads through the wheatfields and vineyards in
the hills surrounding the town of Chablis*

*D*RIVING SOUTH from Paris, the first of the great Burgundian vineyards you reach are those of Chablis; it will be another 100 kilometres before you are within sight of those of the Côte d'Or. The small country town of Chablis is 12 kilometres to the east of the A6 – *Autoroute du Soleil* – near Auxerre. Here and in a few surrounding villages one of the greatest white wines of all is produced. There is nowhere else in the world where the Chardonnay grape – from which Chablis is made – thrives the way it does here on these sunny limestone hills.

While the wine's reputation and importance are immense, the vineyard area where it is produced covers only about 1,500 hectares – and the *Grand Crus* vineyards are limited to about 100 hectares. However, there are more vineyards in the valley of the Yonne, where other types of burgundy are produced.

## THE WINES

Chablis is one of the world's best-known wines and has virtually become a generic term for white wine. The true Chablis is made exclusively from the Chardonnay grape – which is used for all the great white wines of Burgundy. Chablis is crisp and dry, making it the ideal accompaniment to seafood and shellfish; it also has a clear, crystalline quality with a greenish tinge and looks as refreshing and pleasing as it tastes.

There are four classifications of Chablis: *Grand Cru, Premier Cru,* Chablis

*A small private château with an interesting gateway in the village of
Béru to the south east of Chablis*

*Above: A view towards Chablis from a road near the village of Milly*
*Following pages: The attractive village of Chitry, with its fortified*
*church and tower*

and Petit Chablis. Seven *Grand Crus* – Blanchot, Bougros, Les Clos, Grenouilles, Les Preuses, Valmur and Vaudésir – come from the three communes of Chablis, Poinchy and Fyé; the vineyards are on the slopes of the prominent hill immediately to the north east of the town between the D 150 and the D 216. The wines must attain a volume of alcohol of at least 11 per cent and should be kept for at least two or three years; they continue to improve for up to about ten years.

The *Premiers Crus* – there are 27 of these – come from the next most favourably sited vineyards; they have a similar capacity for ageing and must contain at least 10.5 per cent alcohol. Chablis is produced from 19 different communes, the best of the remaining vineyards, while Petit Chablis is from the least favourable terrain and is best drunk quite young.

The production of Chablis is fraught with difficulties, since it is an area prone to spring frosts. Considerable effort is made to combat them. Whenever frost is forecast oil-fired stoves are placed amongst the vines to keep the temperature above freezing point. Another measure involves spraying water from a system of pipes ranged along the vines. The water comes from an artificial lake created specially for this purpose; the principle is that the fine spray of water freezes as it coats the vines and forms a protective barrier of ice.

In addition to Chablis the region is entitled to the appellation Bourgogne and red, white and rosé wines are also made from the Gamay, Pinot Noir and Aligoté grapes. A white wine from the Sauvignon grape is made in the village of St Bris-le-Vineux called Sauvignon de Saint Bris, and just down the road a delightful pale rosé can be found in the village of Irancy, which also makes a light red wine. An interesting red wine is produced in the village of Epineuil, just to the north of Tonnerre.

## THE CUISINE

Gourmets will find all the best influences of Burgundian cuisine in Chablis. The *escargots* are particularly good here; they are often cooked in Chablis. There is a special local *andouillettes à la Chablisienne*, a sausage made from tripe, and the black puddings and pork pies are excellent. Chablis is used in the local, lighter version of *coq au vin* instead of the usual red wine. Ham from the nearby Morvan is a regular feature of menus, as is the magnificent beef of the Charolais. Chablis is also renowned for its meringues, and for its cherries. Among the excellent cheeses found in the region are *Epoisses*, soft and creamy with a dusty reddish coating, and *Saint-Florentin*, similar in appearance but with a stronger flavour; both are made from cows' milk.

## THE ROUTE DES VIN *Michelin map 65*

The Route des Vins in Chablis and the Yonne Valley is not signposted. The route I have suggested takes you to all the most interesting and important

*Above: A jovial* vigneron *rests awhile from the back-breaking task of harvesting the grapes on the steep Beaujolais slopes*
*Left: Set in the attractive little town of St Bris-le-Vineux, this timber-framed house and its pretty window is typical of the region*

villages, mostly along quiet, scenic roads. The town of Chablis is an ideal starting-point for the tour. There are many places where you can sample and buy the wine and, during the summer, the Syndicat d'Initiative mounts a small exhibition of tools, implements, pictures and displays which explain the history and progress of wine-making in the region. A lively market takes place on Sunday mornings, and there is a wine fair on the last Sunday in November. The town itself is small and unassuming with a number of medieval buildings, including the church of Saint-Pierre and the collegiate church of Saint Martin, both dating from the twelfth century.

Leave the town on the D 965 heading towards Auxerre. The first wine village is Milly, high up on the hilly slopes to the west; a small road leads up into the village and its surrounding vineyards. A little further along the main road is the *Grand Cru* commune of Poinchy, designated as a *Village Fleuri* (Flower Village): in the spring and summer every available container – old wine casks, stone troughs, baskets – is crammed with a vivid display of

flowers. Here the route leaves the main road and continues along the D 131 to the village of la Chapelle Vaupelteigne and Villy along the banks of the River Serein. The watermeadows are dotted with the large white Charolais cattle grazing under the trees. Then, on to Maligny, where there is an ancient château in the process of restoration.

From here the route climbs up out of the valley towards Fontenay-près-Chablis and then to Fyé, a *Grand Cru* village in a small valley with the vineyards strung up on the steep slopes about it at a dizzy angle; here you are in the midst of the finest of the Chablis vineyards. Returning briefly to the D 965 and heading towards Tonnerre you come to the wine village of Fleys. Just after this, take the small road to the right which leads to Béru, a charming cluster of ancient grey stone houses. The next village is Viviers, a crumbling hamlet in a small valley. The wine road climbs now to the top of the hill towards Poilly-sur-Serein and, as you drive along, there are wonderful views of the vast, open landscape through which the River Serein weaves its gentle course, the rolling hills patterned with vineyards and grain fields.

The road follows the Serein back towards Chablis through the hamlet of Chemilly-sur-Serein and the attractive small village of Chichée. On the outskirts of Chablis take the D 2 through a small wooded valley to Préhy and then Courgis; these two villages with their vineyards spread around the hill

*The lovely little village church of Préhy set among the hillsides to the south west of Chablis*

*The little town of Irancy, known for its rosé wine, is encircled by hills*
*which are covered with vines and orchards*

slopes mark the western limit of the Chablis vineyards. From here continue along the D 62 towards Chitry, a small town dominated by a fortified church which has a huge round tower. This is the area where the ordinary Burgundy wines are produced. St Bris-le-Vineux, though, makes an unusual dry white wine from the Sauvignon Blanc grape, which is used for the great white wines of Sancerre and Pouilly-sur-Loire, a little further south-west. The wine route here has beautiful and extensive views over the rolling landscape. Next you come to Irancy, situated in an idyllic spot, nestling at the foothills of some steeply sloping hillsides and surrounded by vineyards and orchards; here, a delicate rosé and a light red wine are produced.

From Irancy the wine route continues to the twin towns of Vincelottes and Vincelles, separated by both the River Yonne and the Canal du Nivernais, running side by side. There is a towpath you can walk along and watch the boats and barges making their unhurried progress along the waterways. If you want to stroll further, the road continues alongside the canal to the old town of Cravant.

Now you must back-track a little to Coulanges-la-Vineuse, an appealing village with a mellow old church set in the middle of vine-clad hills. Here the road turns north through the small wine village of Jussy to Vaux, an old stone village set beside the River Yonne. After you cross the river, take the narrow road back towards Chablis, traversing quiet, almost remote countryside, through the hamlets of Augy, Quenne and Montallery. You rejoin the main road, the D 965, at the busy little wine village of Beine, close to the artificial lake that feeds the vineyard sprinkling system; there are many places to sample the wines of the region here. A little road leads up out of the village over the vine-covered hill to Lignorelles. You complete the circuit by returning through Villy and Poinchy to the town of Chablis.

# A Case for Tasting

CHABLIS AND ITS IMMEDIATE NEIGHBOUR to the south-west, the Auxerrois district, form an island of vineyards lying nearer to the Champagne district than to the main part of Burgundy 100 kilometres further south. The wines, accordingly, have a character very much their own.

## CHABLIS

Basic Chablis *appellation contrôlée*, as opposed to the wine from the *Premier* and *Grand Cru* vineyards, enjoys a mixed reputation for quality – much of it being downright bad. But in good vintages such as 1986 and 1988, the best growers, among them William Fèvre of Domaine de la Maladière, do make lively, fresh, 'green-tasting' white wines to drink young.

## CHABLIS PREMIER CRU FOURCHAUME

Fourchaume is among the better of the 27 *Premier Cru* vineyards scattered throughout the region, producing wines of higher concentration and alcohol content than the basic Chablis *appellation contrôlée*. La Chablisienne is a co-operative of about 200 growers, making wines of a uniformly high standard.

## CHABLIS PREMIER CRU MONT DE MILIEU

The big Nuits-St-Georges firm of F. Chauvenet is among the many Burgundy dealers (*négociants*) buying new made Chablis from the growers for 'bringing up' (*élevage*) and bottling under their own label in their company cellars. (Thus the term *Négociant-Eleveur* that appears on so many labels.) Mont de Milieu is among the best *Premier Cru* vineyards, and Chauvenet a reliable firm.

## CHABLIS GRAND CRU LES CLOS

The top wines of Chablis are those from the seven *Grand Cru* vineyards that occupy the slopes looking south over the town across the Serein river. Expensive (150FF is typical) these are 'steely' with acidity but powerfully fruity – to drink when five or more years old. Domaine Vocoret is a leading Chablis firm.

## CHABLIS GRAND CRU GRENOUILLE

The happily named 'Frog' *Grand Cru* vineyard includes the château estate of the same title, from which comes one of the region's greatest wines. The 1986 is beautifully greeny-gold in colour, lushly aromatic and fully fruity but thoroughly elegant in flavour. The wine is distributed by the La Chablisienne co-operative.

## SAUVIGNON DE ST BRIS

While the Chardonnay grape accounts for 100 per cent of Chablis wines, the grape that dominates the nearby St Bris commune of the Auxerrois is the Sauvignon. From a good grower like Luc Sorin, these delicious grassy-fresh white wines can be of superb quality, way above their mere *VDQS* status.

## BOURGOGNE ALIGOTÉ CÔTEAUX DE ST BRIS

In Auxerrois, the Aligoté grape can make a fruity, if rather acidulous dry white wine for everyday low-cost drinking. Curiously, this ordinary wine carries the *appellation contrôlée* designation when made in the St Bris and Chitry districts, whereas the noble Sauvignon is a lowly *VDQS*. Andre Sorin's Aligoté is of reliable quality.

## BOURGOGNE ROUGE CÔTES DE CHITRY

The red burgundy of Auxerrois is all humble *Bourgogne appellation contrôlée*, but largely made with the region's noble Pinot Noir grape. This wine made by Edmond Chalmeau in the Côtes de Chitry was very good in the 1985 and 1986 vintages, with a scent of strawberries, softly fruity and slurpable.

## BOURGOGNE COULANGES-LA-VINEUSE

Another basic red *Bourgogne appellation contrôlée* from the village of Coulanges-la-Vineuse at the St Bris district's southern tip. Sweet-smelling, freshly fruity wines at low cost (around 30FF) to drink within a couple of years of the vintage date.

## JULIUS CAESAR

A St Bris curiosity, this is a *vin de garde* (wine for keeping) made from the black César grape said to have been brought to the region by Julius Caesar's legionaries. The César grape in small quantities gives Irancy reds some of their 'backbone'. On its own it makes a rather tough red to drink after five or more years.

## BOURGOGNE IRANCY

An *appellation contrôlée* wine in its own right, this is the one red wine of the Chablis-Yonne region with any pretentions to international recognition. The stony vineyards of Irancy are claimed by the local growers to make more 'structured' wines, and indeed these reds do have real depth of flavour as well as softly fruity charm. Burgundy's best value red wine at only about 30FF.

## CRÉMANT DE BOURGOGNE BRUT DE BAILLY

Creamily sparkling white and rosé burgundy is a delicious and economic alternative to the costly delights of champagne. Caves de Bailly, the big co-operative at St Bris, makes world-famous *brut* (dry) sparklers from Pinot Noir, Gamay, Aligoté and Chardonnay grapes in an artful blend. At around 35FF, amazing value.

CLOS
DE
TART

Morey St Denis
Centre des Grands Crus

# A Tour of The Côte d'Or

*Above: One of the numerous shops in Beaune which tempt the gourmet*
*with a mouth-watering selection of regional food and wines*
*Left: A sign by the walled vineyard of the Clos de Tart in*
*Morey-St-Denis proclaims its importance on the Côte de Nuits*

ONE OF THE MOST exciting things about exploring the wine roads of France is that every other signpost you encounter seems to carry a familiar and often revered name. This is especially true of the Côte d'Or. You'll see Gevrey-Chambertin, Volnay, Nuits-St-Georges, Montrachet, Vougeot, Meursault, Pommard and Beaune – names that are more familiar in delicate script on the label of a fine bottle of wine – here crudely lettered and scattered casually on roadsigns, walls and plaques.

These famous villages all lie within quite a small area. The Côte d'Or is a ridge of hills that runs almost parallel to the *Autoroute du Soleil*, and the vineyards that pattern its slopes start just south of Dijon and continue in an almost unbroken band to the village of Santenay, some 48 kilometres to the south.

They are divided into two distinctive wine areas; the Côte de Nuits in the northern half, and the Côte de Beaune. The soil here is of a reddish clay with fragments of chalk, with a subsoil rich in minerals. In addition, the disposition of the hills creates an ideal microclimate for the Pinot Noir and Chardonnay grapes, from which the greatest of the Côte d'Or wines are made. This does not mean, however, that winemaking here is a trouble-free occupation. When the first buds appear in April they often have to be protected from hard frosts, while heavy rain in the summer months can easily create the conditions for rot. But the diverse climate and soil in the Côte d'Or

*Above: A view from Orches on the Hautes-Côte de Beaune looking
eastwards over the more prestigious vineyards on the slopes below*

*Previous pages: A winter scene in the vineyards to the west of
Puligny-Montrachet*

mean that there is an extraordinarily rich variety of wine, in terms of
character and quality. Often a distance of only a few hundred metres will be
the difference between a good wine and a really great one: for this reason,
vineyards in the region are called *climats*, since each has its own unique
combination of soil, sun, wind and rain. As a general rule the best wines are
made from the grapes grown on the middle of the slope.

## THE WINES

Red, white and some rosé wines are made here. The great red burgundies of
the region are made from the Pinot Noir grape and the whites from the
Chardonnay. A lesser red wine called *Passe-tout-grains* is made from a mixture
of Pinot Noir and Gamay (the red-wine grape of Beaujolais). In addition, the
Aligoté grape is used for ordinary white wines.

As well as the fine – and expensive – wines from the famous vineyards and
villages of the Côte d'Or there are wines under the appellations Côte de Nuits
and Côte de Beaune, from communes in these general areas; Côte de
Beaune-Villages and Côte de Nuits-Villages from specific communes; and the
Hautes-Côtes de Beaune and the Hautes-Côtes de Nuits from vineyards
higher up in the hills beyond the more famous slopes.

## THE CUISINE

Burgundian cuisine is at its richest and heartiest here and red wine features
strongly in many dishes. This is where *boeuf à la bourguignonne* and *coq au vin*

*A farmhouse surveys the bleak winter scene of vineyards near*
*Chassagne-Montrachet on the Côte de Beaune*

originate. You'll have plenty of opportunities to eat a real *coq au vin* made with
a bird that has spent some time strutting around the farmyard – a far cry from
those made with battery-reared chicken. Red wine is also used in *oeufs pochés en*
*meurette*, eggs poached in a wine sauce. *Gougères* are worth looking out for: they
are light golden mounds of choux pastry cooked with cheese – when eaten hot
the crisp pastry gives way to an oozy, creamy centre. The cheeses include
*Cîteaux*, *Saint Florentin* and *Soumaintrain*, all made from cows' milk.

### THE ROUTE DES VINS *Michelin maps 65 and 69*

The Côte d'Or is divided, geographically and by wine types, into two quite
separate areas – the Côte de Nuits and the Côte de Beaune – although the
vines are virtually continuous. The northern half runs south from Chenôve,
a suburb of Dijon. The distance from Chenôve to Corgoloin, where the Côte
de Beaune route starts, is little more than 24 kilometres. The countryside on
the short northern tour is one you should explore on foot if you have the
time, along the tiny lanes that meander up into the vineyards from the
villages. You will get a fascinating glimpse of the continuing effort that goes
into tending and rearing the vines and, whatever the time of year, something
of interest will be happening in the wine calender.

The Côte de Nuits route starts just outside Dijon, at Chenôve, on the
N 74. It is well signposted, rather proudly, as the Route des Grand Crus.
From Chenôve the wine road follows the D122, a small road that winds its
way up on the gentle slopes of the Côte de Nuits towards the village of
Marsannay-la-Côte, noted for its rosé; it has its own appellation, Bourgogne

Rosé de Marsannay. The next village is Fixin, the first of eight major communes of the Côte de Nuits; in the park just above the village is a bronze statue of Napoleon sculpted in 1846 by François Rude, whose most famous work is the decorative panels of the Arc de Triomphe in Paris.

A few kilometres south is the first of the truly great wine villages of the region, and of the world: Gevrey-Chambertin. Its 3,000 or so inhabitants live in and for the vines, literally; there is a cellar or *cave* underneath most of the houses. Like many other villages on the Côte d'Or, Gevrey has added the name of its most celebrated vineyard, le Chambertin, to its own. There is a second *Grand Cru* vineyard, Clos-de-Bèze, here too. Just to the west of the village is a medieval château restored in the thirteenth century by the monks of Cluny; it has tasting rooms and cellars, a magnificent hall and a grand staircase. On the other side of Gevrey is the Combe de Lavaux, a dramatic wooded gorge where there are excellent picnic spots. The road that leads to it is one of the routes that winds up into the Hautes-Côtes de Nuits.

The next commune is Morey-St-Denis, a quiet village with its famous walled *climat*, the Clos de Tart, which was planted by the Cistercian monks originally, like the vineyards of the neighbouring village Vougeot. There are four other *Grand Cru* vineyards in Morey: Clos de la Roche, Clos St-Denis, Clos des Lambrays and, on the southern border of the commune, Les Bonnes Mares. The wine road now leads to the village of Chambolle-Musigny at the foot of the Côte de Nuits' highest hill. Although, for the most part, they are not particularly beautiful these Burgundian villages have a sense of their own importance; and this small cluster of mellow stone houses surrounded by carefully manicured vines is no exception.

The next village on the wine route is Vougeot, famous for its château and the walled vineyard of Clos de Vougeot, the largest *climat* in the whole of Burgundy. The fine Renaissance château was built by a sixteenth-century abbot at one end of what was already an enormous vineyard; it is said that at one time the French army had to present arms as they passed it. Now the château is the headquarters of the Confrérie des Chevaliers du Tastevin, an organization which promotes the wines of Burgundy throughout the world. There is a wine museum in its huge Romanesque cellars with some interesting medieval wine presses.

The village of Vosne-Romanée and the busy town of Nuits-St-Georges are the last of the great communes on the Route des Grand Crus. The former boasts no less than seven *Grands Crus*. They include Romanée-Conti, which has a reputation for red burgundy that is equalled only by the one Le Montrachet has for its white wine: its scant 2 hectares produce about 3,000 bottles per year. The headquarters of many *négociants-éleveurs* (the merchants who control and market the wine of individual growers) are based in Nuits

*A famous landmark on the Côte d'Or, the gilded mosaic rooftop of the Château of Corton-André in the wine village of Aloxe-Corton*

St-Georges. One of the Apollo astronauts – being a wine lover, or perhaps, a classicist (the ruins of a Gallo-Roman villa were discovered locally) – named a crater on the Moon after the town.

The Côte de Beaune route begins at Corgoloin. One of the first villages you encounter is Aloxe-Corton, a tiny place with few inhabitants and no hotel or restaurant. But it does have two tasting cellars, one in the impressive Château Corton-André (notable for its magnificent gilded

*The mosaic rooftop of the Hospices de Beaune is covered with a dusting of snow in this winter picture*

mosaic roof), and its red and white wines have an international reputation. In the valley that extends westward from the N 74 is the small commune of Pernand-Vergelesses at the foot of the Corton hill. Savigny-lès-Beaune lies only a few hundred metres from the *Autoroute du Soleil* and has a twelfth-century church, two châteaux and many imposing old houses.

And so to Beaune. The capital of the Côte d'Or is a wine town through and through. The leading *négociants-éleveurs* have their headquarters here, and will allow you to tour their vast underground labyrinths of passages and cellars, many dating from the fifteenth century, where the great wines of Burgundy are housed. Beaune has a leafy central square, the Place Carnot, and many lovely old streets, ramparts, a bustling and colourful country market, an abundance of tempting wine and food shops and the Hospices de Beaune, known as the Hôtel-Dieu. Built in 1451 by Nicolas Rolin to house the sick, the Hôtel-Dieu is famous for its steep, brightly coloured, mosaic roof; it is arranged around a magnificent cobbled courtyard and includes an old pharmacy and a museum, where you can see Roger van der Weyden's polyptych of *The Last Judgement*, painted in 1443. Nicolas Rolin also bequeathed his vineyards to the Hospice, and the wine is sold at the auction held every year in the Hôtel-Dieu on the third Sunday in November. Although these wines frequently reach a ridiculously high price, because the proceeds from their sale go to the Hospice and other charities, nevertheless they also usually dictate the sale price of other Burgundian wines. Thus, if a year's prices for the Hospice wines are generally very high, so too will be the prices for the other wines. The auction draws buyers and wine lovers from all over the world and for the three days it lasts called *Les Trois Glorieuses*, not a spare bed is to be found in Beaune or the surrounding towns.

Leaving Beaune and heading south you come to a succession of small villages, all of them famous for their wines – Pommard, Volnay, Monthelie, Auxey-Duresses, Meursault, Puligny-Montrachet, Chassagne-Montrachet and Santenay – and you should spend a few hours in each, sampling the

*The church of St Jean near Santenay on the southern limit of the Côte de Beaune*

*The Château of La Rochepot, restored after damage during the French Revolution, surveys the surrounding countryside from high above the village rooftops*

local products. A small road from Santenay leads to the old church of St Jean which nestles below a rocky outcrop.

You must not miss le Montrachet, the old walled vineyard which produces the world's greatest white wine. It is easy to overlook as there is only a faint inscription on one of the crumbling gateways to signify its presence; it lies mid-way between Puligny-Montrachet and Chassagne-Montrachet, high up on the slopes of the rather stark hill called Mont Rachet, (literally, 'bare mountain'). I was photographing here one bitterly cold January day with snow drifting down on to the vines, when a car stopped and a lightly dressed French couple got out. They gazed reverently at the bleak plot of land for a few minutes. The man was shivering as he turned to get back into his warm car. He caught my eye. '*C'est le Montrachet!*', he said simply.

The vineyards of the Côte d'Or are not only restricted to the prestigious hillsides surrounding these famous villages, and the wine route continues up into the higher terrain known as the Hautes-Côtes de Beaune. Instead of the preened and regimented vines of Pinot Noir and Chardonnay grapes, you see the rather spindly, untidy Aligoté and Gamay, more suited to the less hospitable soil and climate here but not producing such noble wines.

From Santenay you can follow the signs to small villages such as Dezize-lès-Maranges, and then to the top of the Montagne des Trois Croix, where there are stunning views of the Côte d'Or and the Chalonnais. From here the wine road continues through the villages of Sampigny-lès-Maranges and Change, then on towards Nolay on the D 973. Change is an appealing place with many fine old buildings, including an oak-beamed

*Above: Vineyards near Bouze les Beaune close to the Autoroute de
Soleil which, at this point, runs through the Côte d'Or
Right: A village house in Chassagne-Montrachet, Côte de Beaune*

market. Nearby is a spectacular gorge, le Cirque du Bout du Monde, (World's End), where dramatically sheer cliffs surround a peaceful meadow through which a stream wends its way. At the base of the cliff is a waterfall.

The village of la Rochepot is close by; its spired and turreted château was badly damaged during the French Revolution and was restored last century. From here the Route des Hautes-Côtes winds up towards the highest point in the wine-growing area. You go through Orches, stunningly located beside dramatic rock formations; it is also known for its delicate rosé wine. Near the village of Nantoux, follow a narrow road on a detour up the side of a valley, through precariously sited vineyards, over the steep hill and down into the village of Bouze-lès-Beaune.

Further north, over the *Autoroute* towards the small hamlet of Bouilland, the route goes through what is now the Hautes-Côtes de Nuits and continues up steep-sided, wooded valleys towards Marey-lès-Fussey, where the Maison des Hautes-Côtes is situated. This is a centre that promotes the local wines; you can taste and buy them here and eat the regional culinary specialities in the Maison's restaurant.

In these wild and often rugged surroundings, soft fruit, particularly blackcurrants, are grown along with the grapes. Much of the fruit for Cassis, the blackcurrant liqueur for which the region is also famous, is grown here; Kir (named after a former mayor of Lyon who was rather partial to it) is traditionally made with a glass of chilled Bourgogne Aligoté and a dash of Cassis. From here, there's many a lane you can take to get back towards Beaune or the villages along the Route des Grands Crus.

# A Case for Tasting

THE GREAT WINES OF BURGUNDY all come from the vineyards of the Côte d'Or – the 'Golden Slope' that joins the wooded western plateau to the wide, flat valley of the River Saône. The Côte de Nuits is the Côte d'Or's northern half. Red wines from the Pinot Noir grape account for nearly all production.

### NUITS ST GEORGES

Named after the town of the district, this appellation covers red wines typical of the robustly flavoursome style that characterises the Côte de Nuits as a whole. Labouré-Roi is among several famous firms making quality Nuits – best drunk between 5 and 15 years after the vintage date.

### BOURGOGNE HAUTES CÔTES DE NUITS

By Burgundian standards, a humble *appellation contrôlée* for affordable reds (and a very few dry whites), Hautes Côtes wines have plenty of fruit with real Pinot Noir character. Geisweiler & Fils, very large vineyard owners, make this superb Hautes Côtes from their Domaine de Bévy – one of the best vineyards in the appellation.

### CHÂTEAU GRIS NUITS ST GEORGES PREMIER CRU

Château Gris stands in its own 10-acre vineyard within Aux Crots, one of the 38 defined vineyard areas classified *Premier Cru* in Nuits St Georges. Single-estate wines are rare in Burgundy, and Château Gris is a classic, richly coloured and scented red to keep at least ten years before drinking. Both 1987 and 1988 were successful vintages.

### BONNES MARES

A *Grand Cru* vineyard of the famous Chambolle-Musigny village, and a wine of great reputation, especially from a respected firm such as Louis Jadot. Deeply flavoured, elegant burgundy that needs many years of bottle age to reach its peak of drinkability in great vintages such as 1983 and 1985.

### CLOS DE VOUGEOT

The walled vineyard of Clos de Vougeot is the only one in the district of the village of Vougeot classed as a *Grand Cru*. At 125 acres, it is a big vineyard – but it is divided up among 85 different growers! The highly priced (200-300FF) wines are variable in quality, to say the least.

### ÉCHÉZAUX

A *Grand Cru* of the village of Flagey-Échézaux, neighbouring Vougeot. Fine, elegant red wines, but this is one of the vineyards of Burgundy whose reputation has suffered in recent years. The village's other *Grand Cru*, Grands Échézeaux, has a better name. Pierre André's Échézeaux is a good one.

## RICHEBOURG

An opulent-sounding name for a thoroughly opulent wine. Velvety and voluptuous are among the adjectives most often applied to Richebourg, which is one of five *Grands Crus* of the village of Vosne-Romanée. The firm of Jean-Claude Boisset is among the handful offering this very great wine.

## GEVREY-CHAMBERTIN
### Tastevinage

The Gevrey *appellation contrôlée* reds are mixed in quality, but silky and juicily full of fruit when good. The 'Tastevinage' label is awarded to top quality burgundies from throughout the region after annual tastings by the important local wine association, the *Confrérie des Chevaliers du Tastevin*. Only half the wines submitted earn the right of a label.

## ROMANÉE-CONTI

The greatest of the five Vosne-Romanée *Grands Crus*, this pocket vineyard of five acres belongs entirely to the Domaine de la Romanée-Conti, and makes, quite simply, the best red wine in Burgundy. Production is a maximum 7,500 bottles a year and prices are astronomical (at least £200 per bottle at auction for good vintages of recent decades).

## MUSIGNY

Bonnes Mares' *Grand Cru* neighbour at Chambolle-Musigny, and the source of beautiful, smooth red wines with great staying power. Typically 250FF for a young vintage. Do not confuse Musigny with basic Chambolle-Musigny village wines, which are cheaper, but very much less interesting.

## VOSNE-ROMANÉE PREMIER CRU LES MALCONSORTS

The 18 *Premier Cru* sites of Vosne-Romanée are rather overshadowed by their illustrious *Grand Cru* neighbours, but do produce some superb, silky red wines of immense charm at comparatively approachable prices. These are wines to enjoy when at least ten years old. Good vintages include 1985 and 1988.

## VOUGEOT CLOS DE LA PERRIÈRE

From Domaines Bertagna, this is a *Monopole Premier Cru* vineyard from Vougeot – meaning that the entire vineyard is owned by the firm. A supple, elegant red wine with a lighter body than is typical of the Côte de Nuits, this makes an excellent introduction to the region's wine at a price around 100–150FF.

# A Case for Tasting

THE SOUTHERN STRETCH OF THE CÔTE D'OR produces the greatest dry white wines in the world – and a good number of very fine reds, too. Most are famously expensive.

## BEAUNE CLOS-DES-URSULES BEAUNE PREMIER CRU

Clos-Des-Ursules is an individual vineyard owned by the great Beaune firm of Louis Jadot within Les Vignes Franches – one of the 38 *Premier Cru* sites of the Beaune appellation. The red wine is classic, soft Pinot Noir at its best for drinking (from good vintages like 1985) at ten or more years old.

## CHÂTEAU CORTON-ANDRÉ

The hill of Corton is covered by some of the most revered vineyards of the Côte de Beaune. Corton *Grand Cru* is the *appellation contrôlée* for the great red wines – of which Château Corton André is sometimes ranked the greatest. The château stands in the village of Aloxe-Corton at the foot of the hill.

## CORTON-CHARLEMAGNE

This is the name given to the great white wines from the Chardonnay vines on the Corton hill. For a dry wine, it can be amazingly rich and complex in flavour, deepening in colour and flavour with age into a nectareous drink with a wonderful golden hue. Keep at least ten years.

## CHEVALIER-MONTRACHET

One of the celebrated vineyards on the slopes above the villages of Chassagne- and Puligny-Montrachet (*qv*), Chevalier produces white wine of immensely concentrated flavour to keep 10 to 20 years before drinking. 'Les Demoiselles' is a one-acre plot within the vineyard from which Louis Latour makes superb wine – at more than 500FF a bottle.

## BEAUNE HOSPICES DE BEAUNE

Numerous Beaune firms buy wines from the vineyards owned by the town's famous Hospices in the annual auction to raise money for charity. The Hospices have been given 116 acres of vineyards over the last 450 years, and the wines from them now raise more than £1 million a year.

## MEURSAULT

The best-known white burgundy is, at its best, cleanly dry but slightly rich or 'buttery' in texture with spicy undertones in flavour. Even basic 'village' Meursault at under 100FF (as opposed to pricier *Premier Cru* Meursault) can be exotically delicious after a few years in bottle.

## POMMARD

A big village making only red wines, many of them now of a high standard. The first place you reach driving south from Beaune, Pommard's easy-to-pronounce name has made it perhaps more famous than its wines might merit. They cannot always be said to offer the region's best value for money.

## PERNAND-VERGELESSES

It is the village next to Aloxe-Corton, with its own *appellation contrôlée* for much humbler red and white wines. Pernand-Ile-de-Vergelesses is the best vineyard in the village's domain, producing, in the case of this red from the big firm of Moillard, a simple, but good-value Pinot Noir.

## PULIGNY-MONTRACHET PREMIER CRU

Les Folatières is one of 21 *Premier Cru* sites on the revered slopes of beautifully ordered Chardonnay vines rising above the silent village of Puligny. The wines have an exciting balance of clean, arresting acidity and lush, lingering fruitiness of flavour. Drink around eight to ten years old.

## SAINT-AUBIN

An unfashionable *appellation contrôlée* which makes dry white wines of a quality to match some of the grander names. At under 100FF, half the price of the Puligny-Montrachet *appellation contrôlée*, these can be quite deep in flavour with the 'fat' or 'buttery' character that marks fine Burgundy Chardonnay. Recommended bottlers include Prosper Maufoux.

## SANTENAY

A village *appellation contrôlée* in the Côte de Beaune's far south, known for its firmly flavoured reds and a very few whites. Louis Latour, one of Burgundy's top merchant-growers, always offers delicious red Santenays at attractive prices (70–80FF in good vintages such as 1985). Drink from 5 to 15 years.

## VOLNAY PREMIER CRU

Clos des Chênes is among 28 *Premier Cru* sites of the Volnay *appellation contrôlée* surrounding the village of the name lying between Meursault and Pommard. Red wines only, and known for their exceptional fragrance and silky smoothness. Drink at around ten years old. Emile Chandesais's 1987 wine is good value at about 100FF.

# A Tour of The Chalonnais

*Above: A summer scene of vineyards near the wine village of Aluze in the Chalonnais*
*Left: Near the village of St Vallerin to the south of Buxy in the Chalonnais*

ERDS OF BROWN GOATS and the large white Charolais cattle graze peacefully on the gentle slopes and meadows of the Chalonnais, shaded by leafy trees. The atmosphere is relaxed after the self-important bustle of the Côte d'Or. And instead of regimented rows of vines extending as far as the eye can see, here the vineyards are often tucked away out of sight among the other crops.

The Chalonnais is an extension of the Côte de Beaune, separated from it by a narrow strip of vineless countryside. It is a small area in terms of vineyard acreage – smaller even than Chablis – and the vines are less intensively cultivated. The vineyards of the Chalonnais extend south from just beyond Chagny to St Boil, on the D 981, a distance of less than 32 kilometres, and they are seldom more than a few kilometres wide.

## THE WINES

The wines of the Côte Chalonnais are less well known than those of the rest of Burgundy, particularly outside France. However, the grape varieties and the soil have much in common with the more illustrious neighbouring vineyards and, while they do not have the same reputation for character and quality, Chalonnais wines have become more popular, perhaps because the high cost

*Above: Grape pickers at work in the vineyards covering the hillsides to
the west of Rully
Previous pages: The Château of Rully in the Chalonnais where red and
white wines are produced as well as a sparkling Crémant de Bourgogne*

of the better-known wines from Burgundy makes these seem good value. The
four major communes are Rully, Mercurey, Givry and Montagny.

The best white wines are made from the Chardonnay grape and the reds
from the Pinot Noir; however the Aligoté thrives well on this terrain and the
region's Bourgogne Aligoté is highly regarded, in particular that from the
commune of Bouzeron. Sparkling wines are also made here by the *méthode
champenoise*; in addition there is the Bourgogne Passe-tout-grains, a red wine
made from a mixture of Pinot Noir and Gamay grapes.

*An old farmhouse in the small village of Jully les Buxy in the Montagny region of the Chalonnais*

## THE CUISINE

The menus of the Chalonnais are very similar to those of the neighbouring Côte d'Or, with some local variations such as *coquelet au Mercurey* instead of *coq au vin*, and *Charolais au marchand de vin*, a succulent Charolais steak cooked in a red wine sauce with mushrooms and shallots. Among the usual selection of *charcuterie* are a Chalonnais speciality called *rosette*, a spicy saucisson made with red peppers, and *saucisson en brioche*, a spicy pork sausage baked inside a light golden brioche crust. A creamy, mild cows'-milk cheese you will find in the region is *Brillat-Savarin*, a smallish disc with a golden crust named after the nineteenth-century gastronome. There is also *Cîteaux*, a larger cheese with a firmer texture, made from cows' milk. Neighbouring Dijon is famed, among other things, for its mustard, and mustard sauce (*sauce moutarde*) is served often with fish, meat and chicken and of course, with rabbit; the sauce is a creamy combination of Dijon mustard, butter, cream, wine vinegar, egg yolks and stock. You'll also find a special dish of ham and parsley in Dijon, as well as *nonnettes* (iced gingerbread) and *pain d'épice* (gingerbread).

## THE ROUTE DES VINS *Michelin map 69*

The northern gateway to the Chalonnais Route des Vins is the town of Chagny; one of the best restaurants in the region, in the Hôtel Lameloise, is here. You take the D 81 to the first of the four main wine communes, Rully. As you approach the village you will see little evidence of vines, since most of the vineyards are on the hillside behind the village to the west; access is

*Above: A sign denoting the vineyards surrounding the town of Mercury known for its red Chalonnais wines*
*Right: Preparing the barrels during the* vendange *in the Chalonnais village of Bouzeron, known for its Bourgogne Aligoté*

via a narrow road that leads past an imposing château. Although this was a red wine area originally, today the *vignerons* rely mainly on the Chardonnay grape from which they make a fine white wine that is steadily increasing in both quantity and reputation. A white *méthode champenoise* wine, Crémant de Bourgogne, is also made here from the Aligoté grape.

A short detour from Rully will take you back towards Chagny along a narrow country road through unspoiled, almost deserted countryside to Bouzeron, a sleepy little village of ancient stone houses and crumbling farm buildings. It is known for its white wine made from the Aligoté grape: Bourgogne Aligoté. Driving back along the same road on the D 109 you go through a green valley and the small wine village of Aluze, perched precariously on a hill surrounded by vineyards.

From here the Route des Vins continues towards the second of the major wine centres, Mercurey, a one-street town ranged along the D 978. But don't be deceived – Mercurey is, in fact, the largest producer of all the Chalonnais communes. Red wines made from the same Pinot Noir grape as the red burgundies of the Côte d'Or predominate, while a small quantity of white wine from the Chardonnay grape is also produced. There is a tasting cellar where you can sample a variety of these local wines.

As you approach Givry, another important wine town, you'll see signs proclaiming that its wines were Henri IV's favourite tipple. Givry is an old town with a fortified gateway, an ancient covered market, many old houses and a bustling atmosphere; it makes a good base for exploring the region.

Montagny is the most southerly commune of the Chalonnais appellations.

*Above: A sign on a building in the lively small town of Buxy
illustrating the communes of the region
Right: A hilly vine-clad landscape typical of the Chalonnais near St
Mard de Vaux to the south of Mercury*

A peculiarity of the Montagny wines is that the term *Premier Cru* here simply denotes a higher degree of alcohol rather than a superior or specific vineyard, as would normally be the case. This is a white wine area and the vineyards are scattered over the surrounding hillsides, some of which are above 400 metres high.

The quiet, narrow lanes that wind in and around the vineyards offer a succession of rural landscapes and will lead you to some quite delightful small villages. Jully-lès-Buxy is one of them – a picturesque cluster of weathered, golden-stone farmhouses – and the nearby village of St Vallerin is also worth a visit. Buxy, which is larger and busier, has a *cave*, called the Caveau de la Tour Rouge, where you can taste and buy the local wines. Its restaurant serves regional specialities and is attractively situated in an old tower within the remains of the ramparts.

# A Tour of The Mâconnais

*Above: Evening sunlight throws the vineyards into strong relief on the hillsides surrounding the Mâconnais wine village of Lugny*

*Left: Sunshine after a violent summer storm in the vineyards near the village of Fuissé in the Mâconnais*

W INES HAVE BEEN GROWN in Mâcon since Roman times, but it wasn't until a brilliant publicity stunt by a local grower in the seventeenth century that they gained wider recognition: Claude Brosse loaded two casks of his wine on to a cart and travelled for 33 days until he got to the court at Versailles. Louis XIV was very impressed by him – and by his wine, declaring it to be of a better quality than the Loire wines he had been drinking. In recent years the wines of the Mâconnais have become more and more popular and production has increased accordingly.

Although Mâcon itself is the centre of the region's wine trade, the vineyards are situated further to the west, along a line of low hills rising from the valley of the Saône. Coming from the north, it is around Mâcon that your thoughts start turning towards the Mediterranean. The climate is more southerly, the land lush but rugged and the houses have flatter, red-tiled roofs and open-galleried façades. Indeed, the grapes ripen a week or so earlier here than in the more northerly Burgundian vineyards and the harvest takes place correspondingly sooner.

## THE WINES

Although red, white and rosé wines are all made here, the dominant type is white, made mostly from the Chardonnay grape, with a fairly small quantity from Aligoté. The red and rosé wines are made mainly from the Gamay grape, and a little from the Pinot Noir.

*Above: Tractors queue to unload the grapes at the presses of the* cave coopérative *in the Mâconnais village of Vire*

*Previous pages: Vineyards surround the curious pinnacle of rock which crowns the summit of the mountain of Solutré*

The basic classifications of the wines are Mâcon, Mâcon Supérieur and Mâcon-Villages. The difference between the first two is simply that Mâcon Supérieur has a higher minimum level of alcohol. Mâcon-Villages is made from 43 specific communes within the region and the quantity of wine allowed to be produced from each hectare of vines is limited, resulting in better quality wine. In addition there are the named *Crus* from the small region in the south of the Mâconnais; these are Pouilly-Fuissé, Pouilly-Vinzelles, Pouilly-Loché and the most recent appellation, Saint-Véran.

## THE CUISINE

The cuisine of the Mâconnais is typically Burgundian, with all the benefits of the superb ingredients from the surrounding countryside: beef from the Charolais, plump yellow chickens from Bresse and superb *charcuterie*, ham and game, as well as wild mushrooms from the Morvan hills and forests to the north. *Escargots à la bourguignonne* are large, tender Burgundian snails which are simmered in a well-seasoned *court-bouillon* laced with dry white wine, then returned to their shells and stuffed with butter, garlic, shallots, ham and parsley. *Potée à la bourguignonne* is a hearty and sustaining stew made with beef, salt pork, sausage, potatoes, turnips, carrots, cabbage and leeks. Ham is often prepared *à la lie de vin* – in a sauce made from the residues of the wine left in the cask after bottling. The local *andouillettes* and *saucissons* are often served in a sauce made with dry white wine.

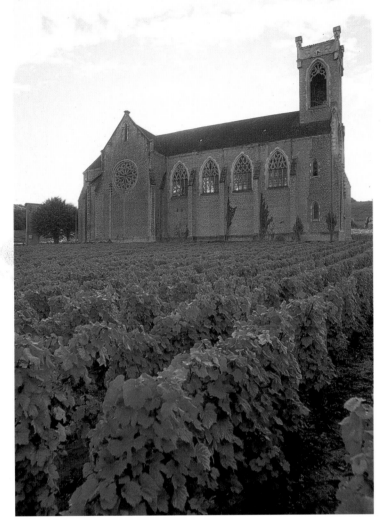

*The village church of Pouilly is virtually marooned among the vineyards which cover almost every inch of precious land in this prestigious area*

## THE ROUTE DES VINS *Michelin maps 69 and 73*

Although the most important wine-growing area is situated immediately to the west of Mâcon, the Route des Vins starts further north, just south of the Chalonnais region beyond Buxy. Drive south on the D 981, a quiet road leading to the heart of the Mâconnais through pleasant, undulating countryside. The first towns you reach are St Boil and Sercy; from the road at Sercy a spectacular château is visible. It is well worth making a short detour to St Gengoux, an attractive medieval town with a twelfth-century château, cobbled streets and many old houses. It also has a good *Cave Co-opérative* where many wines from the Mâconnais and the Chalonnais regions can be tasted. After this, the vineyards become less frequent, but the road is a continuing pleasure with vistas of rolling, wooded landscape. Stop at Cormatin to see the fifteenth-century solid gold Vierge de Pitié in the church. You can also visit the magnificent Renaissance château set in its great park. From here, take the D 14 west towards Ozenay where another turreted château can be seen from the roadside. The vineyards begin in earnest again around the village of Plottes, near Ozenay, on the D 56.

The road continues through a succession of small wine-growing villages, including Chardonnay, Viré, Lugny and Azé. This is gently contoured, open countryside, criss-crossed by quiet lanes. The meadows and fields are planted with grain and vegetables, while the orderly rows of well-tended vines in the vineyards make pleasing patterns.

Many of the villages have wine co-operatives that it is possible to visit. I was in the one at Viré in late September as convoys of tractors towing cartloads of greenish-yellow Chardonnay grapes queued up to deposit their loads. In an atmosphere of busy excitement, I asked how the harvest was this year, and received the true Gallic response – with downturned mouth and shoulders shrugged to the ears – *'Moyen, M'sieu, moyen'* (so-so).

Although the vineyards here are less well known than those of the villages further south, much of the good, honest wine (red, white and rosé) sold under the appellation Mâcon-Villages and Mâcon Supérieur is produced from around these sleepy slopes. Further south is the curiously named town of la Roche-Vineuse, where you should go for a walk up the steep, winding lane via the church to the hilltop, from where there is a superb view of the surrounding countryside.

The real heart of the Mâconnais is a small area just south of the N 79. The villages of Pouilly, Fuissé, Solutré, Vergisson, Davayé, Vinzelles, Loché St-Vérand and Chasselas are clustered almost on top of each other, linked by a number of narrow winding roads. They are all quite small and quiet but are full of character. Then there is the medieval village of St Vérand, which is illuminated during the summer months and looks breathtaking after dusk. In addition to the many individual *vignerons* inviting you to visit their *caves*, there are a number of *Caves Co-opératives* that have a deserved reputation for producing fine wines.

The Route des Vins is well marked but this is hardly necessary, since even an aimless drive in this region will take you to most of the important wine villages. The scenic splendour here is matched by the excellence of the wines: Pouilly-Fuissé is considered by many to be one of the better white wines of France, certainly of the Mâconnais. The vines which produce this great wine

*The distant village of Vergisson shelters under a precipitous crest of rock in the heart of the Mâconnais vineyards*

are planted over a landscape of dramatic character and proportion, dominated by two enormous rocky outcrops, Vergisson and Solutré, cathedral-like as they rise above the vineyards.

The rock of Solutré, a natural fortress, was the gathering place for the Gauls during their final battle for autonomy in 511; a huge bonfire of discarded vines is lit on the summit every Midsummer's Day to mark the event. A vast deposit of prehistoric bones – one layer made up entirely of broken horsebones – was found at the base of the rock in 1866: this site is so important that one period of the Palaeolithic era is now known as Solutrian (18,000 – 15,000 BC). Many of

*Vineyards, meadows and woodland dominate the countryside around
the village of Azé in the north of the Mâconnais*

the archaeological finds discovered here are on display at the Musée des
Ursulines in Mâcon.

Although it is not on the official Route des Vins, it would certainly be a
great pity to bypass the town of Mâcon. Although a busy river port, there is
also a fine old centre where the Maison du Mâconnais, a restaurant serving
the traditional hearty food of the region, and a wine centre are situated.

# A Case for Tasting

THESE TWO SOUTHERN REGIONS OF BURGUNDY are less fashionable than the main Côte d'Or, but nevertheless produce many wines of exciting quality.

### GIVRY

A village in the Mercurey district of the Côte Chalonnaise making lovely, cherry-red Pinot Noir wines and a little white from Chardonnay grapes. Well-made red Givry should have a sweet, berry-like smell and lots of juicy fruit – as Jean Morin's wines do. Drink between five and ten years old.

### MERCUREY

Red wines account for more than 90 per cent of production in the Mercurey *appellation contrôlée*. These are often very good, classic Pinot Noirs with typical cherry-strawberry aroma, rich ruby colour and soft fruit – and typically priced at around 50FF. Best to drink at five to ten years old, and an excellent introduction to red burgundy.

### CHÂTEAU DE CHAMIREY

A grand house with panoramic views over the vineyards of Mercurey, the home of the Marquis de Jouennes is one of the top estates of the region. Lovely, concentrated red Pinot Noir wines and elegant, rich dry Chardonnays are made here. Very good value at under 100FF. Keep the reds at least five years.

### RULLY

The farthest north of the Chalonnais appellations, Rully produces equal quantities of red and white wines. The vineyards reach right to the border with the Côte de Beaune and the wines are said to resemble their very much more highly priced neighbours. Excellent value for money.

### CHÂTEAU DE RULLY

An enormous four-square fortress dating from the thirteenth century looms over the gentle slopes of the vineyard from which this estate takes its red and white wines. The first vintage they made from the new plantings here was the 1986 and the wines are already showing exceptional quality.

### ST-VÉRAN

The neighbouring *appellation contrôlée* to Pouilly-Fuissé, making dry white Chardonnays with great character. The co-operative at Prissé, the village in the region which is also entitled, confusingly, to make Mâcon-Villages wine under its own name, makes a lovely, pale-gold, fruitily refreshing wine.

## MONTAGNY PREMIER CRU

The white Chardonnay wines of this well-known Chalonnais *appellation contrôlée* are characterised by the 'buttery' richness that arises from ageing the wine in oak casks. The Cave des Vignerons de Buxy claims to make 80 per cent of all Montagny *Premier Cru* – which comes from the 60 vineyards entitled to the appellation.

## MÂCON SUPÉRIEUR

Basic Mâconnais wine which reaches 12 degrees alcohol can be labelled *supérieur* rather than plain Mâcon *appellation contrôlée* at a lesser strength. Most *supérieur* is red, made with the Gamay grape and, rarely, a little Pinot Noir, to produce sweet-smelling, light-bodied wines for drinking within five years of the vintage.

## MÂCON-VILLAGES

The 42 villages of the region entitled to this appellation make white wines only, mainly from the Chardonnay grape. The wines are fresh and very drinkable when at their best, with hints of *vanille* from maturation in oak casks. Drink within three years of the vintage.

## MÂCON-CHARDONNAY

Chardonnay is one of the 42 villages and is said to be the source of the name of the Chardonnay grape – thus the strange wording Chardonnay de Chardonnay on this label. (Where the grapes have all come from an individual village *appellation contrôlée*, the label can carry the village's name instead of plain Mâcon-Villages.)

## MÂCON-LUGNY

Another one-village wine. Lugny is among the better known because the renowned Beaune firm of Louis Latour has been making wine here for many years – and the Latour skills really show through. Super-fresh, 'assertive' Chardonnay with lingering flavours. Les Genièvres is the name of the vineyard.

## POUILLY-FUISSÉ

An *appellation contrôlée* just west of the town of Mâcon itself, with a reputation for making grand – and costly– wines. Very often, however, Pouilly-Fuissé seems indistinguishable from decent Mâcon-Villages. Again, the wine is all white from the Chardonnay grape. Drink at about five years old while still fresh with clean acidity.

# A Tour of Beaujolais

*Above: A small chapel crowns the vine-covered hill above the village of Fleurie*
*Left: A small bar-tabac in the golden stoned village of Belmont*

EAUJOLAIS is such a perfect name for a wine – suggesting ruddy cheeked joviality and hearty lust for life – that it might have been thought up by a poetic advertizing executive. In fact, the name is derived from the town of Beaujeu, which lies in the heart of the countryside to the west of the *Autoroute du Soleil*, near Villefranche. The landscape is almost alpine in character with miniature, rounded mountains jostling together, while the country roads wind and climb through them, offering a perpetual display of breathtaking vistas, which is totally captivating.

Protected by the foothills of the Massif Central to the west, the Beaujolais has a mild climate which is ideal for the cultivation of vines, although the mountainous nature of the landscape tends to encourage sudden storms and hail. It is quite a large area, extending from just south of Mâcon to the outskirts of Lyon, and produces a considerable volume of wine – over 11 million cases annually.

## THE WINES

The most important vineyards are situated to the north of Villefranche, where the nine great wine villages of Beaujolais are grouped. In addition to the *Crus*, much of the Beaujolais-Villages wine is also produced from these vineyards. The less geographically favoured communes further south are largely responsible for the production of the basic, unnamed Beaujolais. Beaujolais is a red wine produced from the Gamay grape, and is best drunk young; it is often served lightly chilled. There are five basic types of

Beaujolais. The most common is known simply as Beaujolais; Beaujolais Supérieur merely denotes a higher alcohol content, 10 per cent instead of 9. Beaujolais-Villages is an appellation given to about forty villages in the northern sector of the area and is generally of superior quality to the simple Beaujolais. Beaujolais Primeur, or Nouveau, is a relatively new phenomenon: fermentation is specially controlled so the wine can be bottled and sold – amidst great publicity – by the middle of November. The most prestigious Beaujolais wines are those bearing the name of one of the ten *Crus* Saint-Amour Juliénas, Chénas, Moulin-à-Vent, Fleurie, Chiroubles, Morgon, Brouilly, Côte de Brouilly, and Régnié.

## THE CUISINE

The cuisine in Beaujolais is notable for its simplicity. As elsewhere in Burgundy, the raw materials are of the highest quality, in particular the game from the wooded mountains, the funghi including *morels* and *ceps*, which are found in abundance in the fields and woods, and the pike, carp and trout caught in the Rhône. There are fields of corn and other cereals growing in the valleys of Beaujolais and black truffles are found in the oak forests. The local *charcuterie*, such as *jambon persillé* and *andouillettes*, is the perfect accompaniment to the wines of Chiroubles or Fleurie. The crayfish are justly celebrated and are usually served *à la crème*.

*An autumn scene in the attractive little square of Arbuissonas en Beaujolais*

*Above: Brightly painted shutters and doors are a typical feature of
villages in the southern Beaujolais, this particular house is in Chessy
Following pages: Vineyards covering the hillsides above Beaujeu*

## THE ROUTE DES VINS *Michelin map 73*

The Route du Beaujolais is signposted in a somewhat random fashion, and as you travel the maze of tiny roads you can easily be led into circles of confusion. But it is an agreeable way of becoming confused and the small distances between the villages are such for it not to matter if you become temporarily lost. If you pinpoint exactly where you want to go with the aid of the Michelin map, you can then follow the local signposts to each place. But remember, this is very much a region through which you should meander slowly – even a little aimlessly – in order to appreciate it fully.

It is best to start the Route des Vins at the village of Crêches, near where the Autoroute crosses the N 6, virtually on the border of the Mâconnais and Beaujolais. The division between the two regions is a little blurred here, and you'll see Beaujolais-Villages advertisements for white wines side by side with those for the Pouilly-Fuissé. But look at the vines and you'll know that you are in true Beaujolais country: the tall, gangly vines of the Pinot Chardonnay, from which the white Mâcon wines are made, have given way to the knee-high Gamay vines. Although in other regions the Gamay often produces inferior wines, it is ideally suited to the soil and climate conditions found here.

St Amour-Bellevue is the first village on the wine route. It has a *cave*, called the Caveau du Cru St-Amour, where you can taste and buy the local wines. From here the wine route leads through a succession of the *Crus* wine villages. By and large, they are unremarkable, neither particularly quaint nor picturesque; however, they do have a certain quiet, rural charm and are

situated in quite beautiful settings. They also provide countless opportunities to sample the wines.

In Juliénas, one of the local *caves* is in a deconsecrated fifteenth-century church and the other, just outside the village, is in the Château du Bois de la Salle, headquarters of the local wine co-operative. At the wine-tasting centre in Chénas, the Cellier de Chénas, there is a sculpture by Renoir depicting workers cutting down a forest of oak trees in readiness for planting the vines.

*A derelict farmhouse on the road which leads up to the Col des Truges*

There is scarcely an oak tree to be seen here now. Moulin-à-Vent, where one of the greatest Beaujolais wines is produced, has its tasting cellar close to the vaneless windmill after which the wine is named and which is a famous symbol of Beaujolais. There is a fine restaurant, L'Auberge du Cep serving local food, in Fleurie, as well as an excellent *Cave Co-opérative*.

*A fifteenth-century house in the curiously named village of Oingt, one
of the prettiest of those on the Route des Pierres Dorées*

Of the ten *Crus*, Chiroubles occupies the highest ground, and its vineyards
reach to a height of over 400 metres. If you climb – or drive – up this hill,
past the vineyards, to its summit, you can sample the wines at the tasting
centre and eat the regional specialities in the restaurant while enjoying a
breathtaking panorama over the Haut-Beaujolais. The cellars of Villié-
Morgon, to the south, are also well worth visiting. Here the tasting is done
in the huge vaulted rooms of a château which dates from the fifteenth
century.

Brouilly, south of the D 37, boasts two wine châteaux – Château de la
Chaize and Château de Pierreux – and two *Crus*: Brouilly is made in six
different villages, while Côte de Brouilly comes from the vines that grow on
the sunny southern slopes of Mont Brouilly. On the first Sunday in
September a procession winds its way up the mountain to the small chapel
of Notre Dame du Raisin on the summit, and there they pray for a successful
harvest.

Between Chiroubles and Brouilly make a detour via the Col du Truges
and the Col du Fût to Beaujeu. The route is one of the most spectacular in
the Beaujolais, with narrow tracks winding along the hillsides by steep
plunging valleys at times reminiscent of the roads of Austria and
Switzerland. Further south, beyond Brouilly, is Vaux-en-Beaujolais, the
village where Gabriel Chevalier set his novel *Clochemerle*. Predictably, an
*auberge* and a tasting cellar honour the connection.

The charms of Beaujolais are not limited to the northerly vineyards and
the famous nine villages. The region to the south of Villefranche mainly
produces ordinary Beaujolais; and it has much else to offer the traveller.

There is a signposted route, called the Route des Pierres Dorées, which leads through beautiful unspoilt countryside to a succession of enchanting golden-stone villages. It begins at Limas, a small suburb of Villefranche. From here the D 70 climbs up along the ridge of a hill towards the village of Charnay; there are wide, sweeping views to the east over the Saône and further to the north towards Beaujeu. A little further along is Belmont, which in spring and summer is always bedecked with flowers. These villages look very different from those of the more affluent communes not many kilometres north. There are plenty of places along the route where you can stop to taste and buy the simple wines produced here by an apparently limitless number of individual growers.

Châtillon, Chessy and Bagnols, three more small villages within a very small area, are well worth a brief detour; they are quiet, unspoilt and apparently completely unaware of their charm – always an endearing quality. The road north from le Bois-d'Oingt towards Oingt is another route with beautiful views over the diverse landscape. Oingt is walled and has narrow cobbled streets and many honey-coloured houses; there are a number of craft workshops in the streets, a wine-tasting cellar, an old tower and a terrace beside the church with fine views of the surrounding countryside. More obviously 'picturesque' than many of the other villages, it is also more self-conscious.

This part of the Beaujolais is a virtual maze of tiny roads leading to innumerable small villages; a fascinating area to explore. However remote it seems, at no time are you far from the main road, the D 485, which takes you to Lyon, back on to the *Autoroute du Soleil*, or further west towards Roanne and Clermont Ferrand and the vineyards of the Auvergne.

*One of the wooden sleds which are used to haul the baskets of harvested grapes up the steep slopes of the Beaujolais vineyards*

# A Case for Tasting

WHILE HALF THE HUGE BEAUJOLAIS HARVEST goes into the annual production of Nouveau wine, the region does produce much other – and very much more interesting – wine besides.

## BEAUJOLAIS APPELLATION CONTRÔLÉE

Everyday Beaujolais can be very ordinary stuff, but from a top-class grower like Jean Garlon it is a scintillatingly fresh and zesty red wine of the thoroughly slurpable type. Definitely a wine to drink young, to enjoy the character of the Gamay grape at its youthful best.

## BEAUJOLAIS NOUVEAU

Between 1970 and 1990, sales of Beaujolais Nouveau worldwide have risen from 13 million to 80 million bottles annually. The newly made wine varies in quality from year to year, and no maker is entirely consistent in standard. What is always the case, though, is that the wine does not have to be drunk in the first week – it keeps perfectly well until the following spring.

## BEAUJOLAIS-VILLAGES

All in the northern sector of the region, there are 31 communes entitled to label their wine Beaujolais-Villages *appellation contrôlée*. The wines, from the granitic soil of the north, have a little more body and concentration than basic Beaujolais, but should still be drunk within two years of the vintage.

## CÔTE DE BROUILLY

One of the ten individual communes entitled to their own *appellation contrôlée*. In effect these are single-village wines, each with its own characteristics. Côte de Brouilly wines are quite full and juicy with real intensity of flavour. To drink between two and ten years old. Domaine de la Pierre Bleue was very good in 1987.

## CHÉNAS

Another, and the smallest, of the ten *Crus* as the individually ranked communes are known, Chénas gets its name from the fact that its vineyards were once a forest of oak trees (*chênes*). The wines, including Jacques Depagneux's good Domaine de Chassingnol, are soft and rich and will improve for six or so years.

## CHIROUBLES

A *Cru* in the lighter style of Gamay wine, but famous for its seductive fragrance of violets. Chiroubles is delicious at two or three years old, but the best ones such as those from the respected Cellier des Samsons will age very well. A small *Cru*, and not always an easy wine to find.

—74—

## FLEURIE

Silky smooth and elegant, the wine of Fleurie is now very fashionable, and becoming relatively expensive (50FF for good examples). Its aroma has been described as 'fresh, floral' one of 'rose, iris, violet and peony'! Wonderful wine, especially from Château des Capitans, to enjoy anywhere from 2 to 15 years old.

## JULIÉNAS

Like Fleurie, a *Cru* with a wonderful scent – this time of raspberries and strawberries. Powerfully flavoured Gamay with a fine, deep-purple colour, this is a good Beaujolais to enjoy with food. Best within five years. Domaine des Berthets was an outstanding wine in 1987.

## MORGON

The meatiest and most robust of the *Crus*. Deep garnet in colour and with a 'backbone' uncharacteristic of most Beaujolais, Morgon transforms over a few years in bottle from a recognisable Gamay base into a wine that tastes distinctly like Pinot Noir. Very good years such as 1985 will keep two decades.

## MOULIN À VENT

Named after a 300-year-old, sailless windmill outside the village of Romanèche-Thorins, this *Cru* shares the long-keeping characteristics of Morgon. It is rich and smooth in style, and needs keeping for three or so years before opening. When young it has a lovely deep ruby colour. A wine to buy early, and drink late.

## SAINT-AMOUR

Romantically named, this *Cru*'s wines are often appropriately described as 'charming'. While young, the wine is lushly fruity and intense in the best Gamay tradition, but it ages well too, into a mellow, round red of real character. It is the northernmost of the *Crus*.

## BEAUJOLAIS BLANC

Not all Beaujolais is red Gamay. A tiny quantity – about half a per cent of total production – is white, made mainly from the classic Chardonnay grape. Louis Jadot's Beaujolais Blanc is dry but richly fruity with a broad hint of that 'buttery' character of Côte d'Or wines that comes from maturing in oak casks.

# Wine Buying Guide

## CHABLIS AND THE YONNE

This region's name is so well known that it is copied in other vineyards outside the protective legislation of the European Community. This worldwide fame has led to steep increases in prices over the past few years as demand has outstripped harvest yields. This means that Chablis wines, although quite delicious, no longer represent very good value for money.

### APPELLATIONS CONTRÔLÉES

*Chablis Grand Cru* The seven *Grand Cru* vineyards are arranged on slopes between the town of Chablis itself and the village of Fyé. The same slopes also grow the grapes for Chablis Moutonne, a brand name owned by Joseph Drouhin which, although not a *Grand Cru* itself, is acknowledged as being of similar standard.

The *Grands Crus*, particularly in good years, must be given three or four years' bottle ageing to show their true colours.

*Chablis Premier Cru* Of the 27 *Premier Cru* vineyards, perhaps the most famous are Fourchaume, Vaulorent, Montée de Tonnerre, Monts de Milieu, Vosgros, Vaugiraud, Monts Mains, Les Fôrets, Vaillons and Côte de Léchet.

These wine are less intense than the *Grands Crus* but still need two or three years in bottle to develop. Here, perhaps, the biggest influence on quality is the method of vinification, namely whether oak casks or stainless steel vats are used.

*Chablis* The general appellation of the district covering the remaining vineyard area. This

*The Burgundian castle of Château Rapatous is set among vineyards in a shallow valley below the attractive old town of Theize*

wine is of slightly weaker alcohol content than the *Premiers* and *Grand Crus*.

*Petit Chablis* The most humble wine of the appellation.

### OTHER APPELLATIONS CONTRÔLÉES

*Bourgogne Aligoté* A dry white wine made from the less noble Aligoté grape throughout the entire Burgundy region but only allowed this appellation. In the Chablis area it produces a particularly crisp wine that is delightful to drink locally but is less interesting if taken home.

*Bourgogne Irancy* Red and rosé wine made from the Pinot Noir grape and local varieties César and Tressot. The rosé is better than the red because in poor years ripening is a problem and the wine is thin and stalky.

### VDQS

*Sauvignon-St-Bris* A white wine only, making an excellent apéritif. Drink as young as possible.

### GENERIC APPELLATION CONTROLÉE COVERING ALL BURGUNDY INCLUDING YONNE

*Bourgogne Rosé* Made from Pinot Noir, César and Tressot grape varieties, but not common now.

*Crémant-de-Bourgogne* A white or rosé sparkling wine made by the *méthode champenoise* throughout the Burgundy region. Like *crémant* in Champagne, this has two-thirds the normal $CO_2$ pressure.

### VIN DE PAYS

*Vin de Pays de l'Yonne* Light, dry white wines only.

In the town of Chablis there is a wine shop belonging to Domaine Laroche where you can see a full range.

## THE COTE D'OR

The two districts of the Côte d'Or are markedly different. The Côte de Nuits produces very little white wine, and its reds are masculine with more colour, tannin and backbone than those of the Côte de Beaune.

The wines of the Côte de Beaune are both red and white. Here, stretched between Fixin and Santenay, are most of the great names of Burgundy. Some village communes are more noble and so better known than others.

The problem in purchasing is quantity. The well-known names have to satisfy a worldwide demand for their production and this means that some wines are sold at prices well beyond their actual worth. Even in the area it is impossible to buy the great wines cheaply. The generic appellation wines such as Bourgogne Rouge or Blanc often offer the best value. If purchased from a *négociant* skilled at blending or from an individual grower, these wines can be excellent even if you forgo the possibility of pinpointing the vineyard of production on a map.

### CRU CLASSIFICATION SYSTEM

The vineyards of Burgundy are divided first into village communes and then into individual patches called *climats*. Each *climat* has its own soil and microclimate conditions and so produces its own unique wine. Because of the historical inheritance laws in Burgundy, whereby each child had an equal share in his father's estate, the vineyard holdings have become broken up. Nowadays, through intermarriage and the purchase of vineyard plots, people owning a *domaine* may well have several separate plots within many *climats* spread over several village communes.

Of these *climats*, those producing the most superior wines are designated *Grand Cru*. These *climats* are so well known that they do not need to use the village name on the wine label. Indeed, a village often annexes the name of such a *climat* to its own to develop more self-importance. Thus the village of Gevrey became Gevrey-Chambertin.

Other very good *climats* are designated *Premier Cru*. The *Premiers* and *Grands Crus* form a belt occupying the best parts (the middle) of the Côte d'Or slope. Lesser *climats* are given over to producing lesser wines within the village commune appellation.

Here is an example from the commune Gevrey-Chambertin.

*Chambertin* A *Grand Cru* wine from the Le Chambertin *climat*.

*Gevrey-Chambertin* Clos St Jacques. A *Premier Cru* wine from the Clos St Jacques *climat*.

*Gevrey-Chambertin Premier Cru*. A blend of wines but only from *Premier Cru climats*.

*Gevrey-Chambertin* The village wine blended from anywhere within the commune.

NB Wines from the commune of Gevrey-Chambertin may not be declassified to Côte-de-Nuits-Villages.

It is fairly common for a *Grand Cru climat* to be shared between two communes.

## THE CÔTE DE NUITS

**APPELLATIONS CONTRÔLÉES**

Rather than list the wines in order of classification it is perhaps best to discuss them in geographical order from north to south.

*Marsannay-la-Côte* A small amount of red wine is produced as Bourgogne Rouge, but it is the rosé, Rosé de Marsannay, that this commune is famous for.

*Fixin* A small village commune with no *Grands Crus* and only six *Premier Cru climats*: Les Meix-Bas, Le Clos-du-Chapitre, Aux Cheusots, La Perrière, Les Arvalets and Les Hervelets. Although white wines are allowed only red is made. It can be quite long-lived.

*Brochon* This commune only produces lesser wines not sold under the commune name but contributing to Bourgogne Rouge and Côte-de-Nuits-Villages blends.

*Gevrey-Chambertin* A big commune with two major *Grands Crus*: Chambertin and Chambertin-Clos-de-Bèze, which are surrounded by the other *Grands Crus* of Charmes-Chambertin (also called Mazoyères-Chambertin), Chapelle-Chambertin, Griotte-Chambertin, Latricières-Chambertin, Mazis-Chambertin and Ruchottes-Chambertin. All are rich reds needing several years' ageing.

The *Premiers Crus*, which may put their name after the words Gevrey-Chambertin, number 25 of which the best known are Clos St Jacques, Aux-Combottes and Combe-aux-Moines.

Even the commune wine, Gevrey-Chambertin, can be outstanding.

*Morey-St-Denis* The *Grands Crus* are Bonnes-Mares (part of which is also in neighbouring Chambolle-Musigny), Clos-St-Denis, Clos-de-la-Roche and Clos-de-Tart. There are 26 *Premier Cru climats* of which the best known are Clos Bussière and Les Fremières. Again, Morey-St-Denis also makes an excellent village wine.

*Chambolle-Musigny* The *Grands Crus* are Le Musigny (divided into Les Petit Musigny and Les Musigny) and the remaining part of Bonnes Mares. A little white Musigny exists and is well worth finding, but it will be expensive.

There are 20 *Premier Cru climats* of which the best known are Les Charmes and Les Combottes (not to be confused with Aux-Combottes in Gevrey-Chambertin).

Again, the village wine, Chambolle-Musigny, can also be quite outstanding.

*Vougeot* The only *Grand Cru* is Clos-de-Vougeot, the largest single *climat* in Burgundy with 52 hectares. In one corner is the Château de Vougeot, the headquarters and meeting place for the *Confrérie des Chevaliers du Tastevin*, founded in 1933. This *climat* accounts for the majority of the vineyard of the commune, but there are four *Premiers Crus* which are not often seen. Some white wine also exists in the *Premier Cru climats*. Even the village wine is rare because the remaining vineyard area of the commune is much smaller than the *Grand Cru*.

*Flagey-Échézaux* This commune used to be considered as part of Vosne-Romanée, but in fact it is

*To the north of Beaune on the Côte d'Or, the gilded church spire of Pernand-Vergelesses shines above the village rooftops*

a commune in its own right. Displaced about 1 kilometre to the west of the village are the *Grands Crus*; Grands Échézaux and Les Échézeaux. The only *Premier Cru climat*, Les Beaux-Monts, is shared between this commune and the neighbouring Vosne-Romanée. The wine is red only.

*Vosne-Romanée* The *Grands Crus* are La Romanée-Conti, Le Richebourg, La Romanée, La Tâche and Romanée-St-Vivant. Perhaps the most important *domaine* here is the Domaine Romanée-Conti, which has holdings in all these *Grands Crus*, and is owned jointly by Mme Bize-Leroy and A.P. de Villaine. There are two *Premiers Crus* of which the best known are Les Suchots and Aux-Malconsorts. There is also the excellent village wine of Vosne-Romanée.

*Nuits-St-Georges* A large, well-known commune with no *Grands Crus* but 29 *Premiers Crus*. The best known of these are Les-Saint-Georges, Aux-Damodes, Aux-Champ-Perdrix and La Perrière (not to be confused with the *climat* of the same name in Fixin). Some of the *Premiers Crus* are actually in the adjacent commune of Prémeaux (see below).

A white wine does exist in this commune but it is extremely rare.

*Prémeaux* This is in fact a separate commune but all its *Premiers Crus* are classified as Nuits-St-Georges. The best known are Clos-de-la-Maréchale, Clos Arlots (where the rare white is grown), Aux Perdrix and Clos-des-Fôrets. There is no village wine of Prémeaux.

### GENERIC APPELLATIONS

*Côte de Nuits-Villages* This is a general appellation that can be blended from several communes of the Côte de Nuits; Fixin, Brochon, Prissey, Comblachien and Corgoloin. Wines from the other communes mentioned

above may never be sold as Côte de Nuits-Villages. This appellation exists for both red and white wines but in fact is predominantly red.

*Hautes Côtes de Nuits* An appellation covering blends from the less good upper slopes of the Côte and Arrière Côte to the West.

## THE CÔTE DE BEAUNE

### APPELLATIONS CONTRÔLÉE
*Ladoix-Serrigny* This appellation makes red and white wines under the names Ladoix Rouge and Ladoix Blanc. The white is by far the superior. There are two rare *Grands Crus*; Les Vergennes (part is only rated *Premier Cru*) and Le Rognet-Corton (often deemed to be a *Grand Cru* of neighbouring Aloxe-Corton). The six *Premiers Crus* are also rare, and these too are deemed to belong to Aloxe-Corton.

*Aloxe-Corton* This commune has the famous *Grand Cru* red wine Corton (shared with neighbouring Pernand-Vergelesses), subdivided into Le Corton, Corton-Clos-du-Roi, Corton Renardes, Corton-les-Bressandes and Corton-les-Perrières, among others. There are also two *Grands Crus* producing only white wines; Charlemagne and Corton-Charlemagne (part of which is also in neighbouring Pernand-Vergelesses).
There are eight *Premiers Crus* making mostly red wine with a tiny amount of white. The village wine is both red and white.

*Pernand-Vergelesses* This commune shares the white *Grand Cru* Corton-Charlemagne and the red Corton with Aloxe-Corton. It also has five *Premiers Crus* of which the best known is Ile-des-Vergelesses. The wines are both red and white and tend to be a bit harder and firmer than their neighbours.

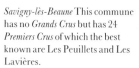

*Savigny-lès-Beaune* This commune has no *Grands Crus* but has 24 *Premiers Crus* of which the best known are Les Peuillets and Les Lavières.

The wines in this commune are red and quite light and soft. There is no white.

*Chorey-lès-Beaune* This small commune only produces a village wine. It is mostly a soft, light red; there is no white.

*Beaune* Despite its worldwide fame, this large commune has no *Grands Crus*. Of the 34 *Premiers Crus* the best known are Le Clos-des-Mouches, Clos-du-Roi, Les Cents Vignes, Les Grèves, Les Marconnets, Les Teurons and Les Vignes-Franches. The *Premiers Crus* make mainly red wines but the white exists in reasonable quantities. Beaune *Premier Cru*, a blend of more than one *Premier Cru climat*, is quite common. There is also a straight village wine and a small area with a separate appellation, Côte de Beaune, making red and white wines. Do not confuse this with the name for the whole district or the appellation, Côte de Beaune-Villages.

*Pommard* Again, a famous commune with no *Grands Crus*. Of the 26 *Premiers Crus* the best known are Les Épenots and Les Rugiens. This commune makes only red wine.

*Volnay* No *Grands Crus* but 27 *Premiers Crus* of which the best known are Les Caillerets, Taille-Pieds and En Chevret.

This commune also produces red wine in the lighter, more rounded style.

(Note that Volnay-Santenots is in fact in Meursault: see Meursault.)

*Monthélie* A small commune to the south-west of Volnay with 11 *Premier Cru climats*, all bordering Volnay or Auxey-Duresses to the south. It produces mostly red wine. This appellation deserves to be better known, but at the moment its obscurity means that its wines are excellent value.

*Meursault* A large commune with no *Grands Crus* but 21 *Premiers Crus*, of which the best known are Le Poruzot, La Goutte d'Or, Les Genevrières and Les Charmes. The commune produces mostly white wines but also some red.

Where a *Premier Cru climat* produces a red wine it has to borrow the neighbouring village's name because there is no appellation for red *Premier Cru* Meursault. Thus Volnay-Santenots and Blagny La-Pièce-sous-le-Bois are in fact red wines produced by *Premier Cru climats* in Meursault.

The white wines are rich and full.

*Blagny* This tiny commune does produce a village wine under its own name, but the *Premier Cru climats* come under Meursault when they produce white wines (see Meursault). The wines can be sold as Meursault-Blagny, Puligny-Blagny or as one of the Meursault *Premiers Crus* if from the *climats* La Jennelotte, La Pièce-sous-le-Bois or Sur-le-Dos-d'Ane.

*Auxey-Duresses* This commune makes both red and white wines of good quality but of less intensity than those of neighbouring Mersault. There

are no *Grands Crus* but eight *Premiers Crus* including Les Duresses (shared with Monthélie) and Les Grands Champs. Prior to the advent of *Appellation Controlée* law these wines were sold as Volnay and Pommard without diminishing the reputations of those two wines.

*St-Romain* A tiny commune up the slopes from Auxey-Duresses and Meursault making only a village wine. The wine is mostly white, and only rarely red. The white wine can be extremely good value when compared to the price of its neighbours.

*Puligny-Montrachet* This commune shares the white wine *Grands Crus* of Le Montrachet and Bâtard-Montrachet with Chassagne-Montrachet but also has the white *Grands Crus* of Chevalier-Montrachet and Bienvenues-Bâtard-Montrachet.

Le Montrachet is the pinnacle of white Burgundy and is regarded by many as France's finest white wine.

There are 11 *Premier Cru climats* making mostly white wine of which the best known are Les Folatières and Les Combettes.

The straight village white wine is also very fine and the red is interesting but quite rare.

*Chassagne-Montrachet* This commune shares the *Grands Crus* of Le Montrachet and Bâtard-Montrachet with Puligny-Montrachet, but also has the tiny Criots-Bâtard-Montrachet.

There are 12 *Premiers Crus* making both red and white wines, of which the best known are Clos-St-Jean and Abbaye-de-Morgeot.

The village wine is also good in both red and white and is a little fuller than neighbouring Puligny-Montrachet.

*St Aubin* This small commune, to the west of Chassagne-Montrachet, produces red and white wines. There are eight *Premier Cru climats*.

*Checking the progress of the new wine in the cellars of Santenay in the Côte de Beaune*

*Santenay* This commune has seven *Premiers Crus climats* producing both red and white wines of which the best known are Les Gravières and La Comme.

The red wines of Santenay are lighter and softer than most in the Côte de Beaune. The whites are fuller and can be quite delicious.

*Cheilly, Dezize and Sampigny-lès-Maranges* These are lesser communes around the end of the Côte de Beaune. Between these three appellations there are four *Premier Cru climats* of which one, Les Maranges, is shared by all three communes.

**GENERIC APPELLATIONS**
*Côte de Beaune-Villages* This appellation is only for red wine blended from all the above communes except Aloxe-Corton, Pommard and Volnay. It is usually light and fruity and can be drunk relatively young.

*Hautes-Côtes de Beaune* A lesser *Appellation Controlée*, blended from the top of the Côte and the Arrière Côte.

## THE CHALONNAIS

This region, also called La Région de Mercurey, consists of scattered vineyards spread among areas of other agricultural activity. Until the 1970s these wines were not exported to the UK and they are still not as well known as they deserve to be.

Although lacking the class of the Côte d'Or wines, the Chalonnais wines have a lightness and fruitiness that makes them attractive in their own right. Those from good years, after two or three years in bottle, can be confused with more famous appellations, which makes them good value. The village of Bouzeron, around which the best of the Bourgogne Aligoté is grown, is in this region.

The *Cave Co-opérative* at Buxy also makes very good generic wines as well as wines from the four main appellations.

**APPELLATIONS CONTRÔLÉES**
*Rully* Predominantly white wines are produced here although the red does exist in tiny quantities.

There are 19 *Premier Cru climats* but these in no way match the *Premiers Crus* of the Côte d'Or. Much of the production here is used to make Crémant de Bourgogne.

*Mercurey* This commune makes almost entirely red wine. The white is very rare. There are five *Premier Cru climats* producing what is generally judged to be the finest red of the whole region.

*Givry* Another commune producing predominantly red wine. The wines are pleasantly fresh and fruity, and are surprisingly good value. They can be drunk quite young.

*Montagny* Produces mostly a white wine that is regarded as the best of the region.

The Beaune shipper, Louis Latour, led the way with this appellation and now most merchants list it. In good vintages, such as 1983, this wine will develop a lovely *goût de miel* (honey-taste).

**GENERIC APPELLATIONS**
*Bourgogne Passe-Tout-Grains* Red or rosé wines made from a mixture of two-thirds Gamay grapes and one-third Pinot Noir. This *Appellation Controlée* is found throughout Burgundy but is mostly produced in the Chalonnais and Mâconnais regions.

## THE MACONNAIS

Although the countryside here is more dramatic, the wines are not as good as those of the Chalonnais or the Côte d'Or districts. All the reds and some of the whites within the appellation are sold without geographical origin.

**APPELLATIONS FOR RED WINE**
*Mâcon Rouge and Mâcon Supérieur* Essentially these are fairly pedestrian wines, a cut above *vin ordinaire*, but they are widely known and popular as everyday wines. Coming mostly from the Gamay grape, but with some Pinot Noir, these wines tend to be more earthy and rustic than the wines of Beaujolais. *Supérieur* just indicates an extra degree of alcohol.

**APPELLATIONS FOR WHITE WINE**
*Pouilly-Fuissé, Pouilly-Loché and Pouilly-Vinzelles* Pouilly Fuissé is the most famous white wine of the region, produced to the west of the villages of Pouilly and Pouilly-Solutré. This wine has recently become fashionable with Americans and their avid purchasing has caused almost incredible price rises. The wine now fetches nearly as much as the whites in the Côte de Beaune and no longer represents value for money. However, the very similar neighbouring wines Pouilly-Loché and Pouilly-Vinzelles, made from the same Chardonnay grape, are still worth finding. A visit to the Caves des Grands Crus Blancs at Vinzelles would be very rewarding.

*St-Véran* This is a new appellation changing its name from Beaujolais Blanc in 1971. The boundaries between Mâcon and Beaujolais are sufficiently indistinct to have allowed this to happen. This white wine is produced from seven communes around Fuissé towards St Vérand. It is still relatively unknown and so is very good value.

*Individual Mâcon village wines* The appellation Mâcon-Villages is only for white wine blended from any of the 43 communes entitled to use the appellation. Some of these villages make a classier, more individual wine and are therefore entitled to use their name after the word Mâcon.

Mâcon-Lugny, Mâcon-Clessé, Mâcon-Prissé and Mâcon-Viré are among the best known. Not so well known but still worth finding are Mâcon-Ige, Mâcon-Uchizy and the rare Mâcon-Fuissé.

An excellent white Mâcon is made at the Château de Chaintré.

*Mâcon Blanc* The more ordinary wines go under this generic appellation, but generally Mâcon Blanc is better than Mâcon Rouge.

## BEAUJOLAIS

The largest viticultural district of Burgundy is Beaujolais accounting for two-thirds of the region's production. However, the Beaujolais district is very different from the rest of Burgundy viticulturally, climatically and oenologically. The scenery is rural and quite beautiful and its character is matched by the liveliness and fruitiness of the wines.

When tasting from the distinctive glasses (shaped like brandy glasses) that are used in the district, look for assertive wines with good fruit, acidity and tannin, and if you want a keeping wine, ask for a *vin de garde*.

**APPELLATIONS CONTRÔLÉES**
In the northern half of the district are ten parishes, each allowed to use its own name, which produce the better wines known as Crus Beaujolais: *St-Amour, Juliénas, Chénas, Moulin-à-Vent, Fleurie, Chiroubles, Morgon, Brouilly, Côte-de-Brouilly* and *Régnié*. Most benefit from keeping for two to three years, especially in good vintages. Moulin-à-Vent, Chénas and Morgon are thought to keep the longest. When these wines age, they lose their purple colour, freshness and fruitiness and start to resemble Pinot Noir wines from more noble appellations.

*Beaujolais-Villages* This wine is red only. It is blended from 39 communes in the north of Beaujolais, including the nine *Crus* and some communes in the hazy Beaujolais/Mâconnais border. The wines must have the same alcoholic strength as Beaujolais Supérieur (10°). The quality is usually above average and, if skilfully blended, can be better than a poorly made *Cru*.

*Beaujolais Supérieur and Beaujolais* These appellations cover the rest of the district. Only about 1 per cent of the production is white, with an equally tiny proportion of rosé. Beaujolais Supérieur must have one degree of alcohol more than straight Beaujolais but in both appellations the quality can and often does vary enormously.

**VDQS**
*Coteaux du Lyonnais VDQS* Red, dry white and rosé wines produced around Lyon, to the south of Beaujolais. The whites are the rarest.

# Museums and Châteaux

*When opening times are not stated it would be advisable to phone before starting out.*

## CHABLIS-YONNE

### WILLIAM FÈVRE

One of a number of Chablis wine producers with grand premises in the town which are open to the public, and offer direct sales. You enter the imposing 19th-century *caves* via an archway adorned with a curious rectangular clock bearing the motto *Da laborem dabo fructus* ('Give me your labour, I give you my fruits'). Fèvre produces some of the very best Chablis wines, from just about every one of the top-rated vineyards.
*14 Rue Jules Rathier, 89800 Chablis.*
*Tel (86) 42–12–51.*

### CHÂTEAU DE MALIGNY

An 18th-century rebuild of the 12th-century feudal original, this atmospheric castle has an unusual quirk about it – for it is built not atop a hill as fortresses are supposed to be, but down in the valley, complete with gardens running down to the River Serein. Now being restored by owner Jean Durup, a celebrated Chablis winemaker, one of whose wines is marketed under the label Château de Maligny, the castle has some beautifully furnished rooms well worth seeing.
*Maligny, 89800 Chablis.*
*Tel (86) 47–44–49.*

### CAVES DE BAILLY

At this major Auxerre co-operative, the wines are made and matured in an extraordinary labyrinth of caves cut into the hills overlooking St Bris. The 12ft-high caverns are the excavations made in quest of the finest limestone – dating back to the 12th century. Some of France's greatest buildings are constructed with stone from here, including the Louvre and the Sacré Coeur in Paris. You can buy the excellent Crémant de Bourgogne and other fine Bailly wines in the adjoining shop.
*BP 3, 89530 St Bris-Le-Vineux. Tel (86) 53-34-00.*

## COTE D'OR

### CHÂTEAU DU CLOS DE VOUGEOT

Driving along the Route des Vins towards Nuits St Georges, you get unmissable views to your left of the massive Renaissance château, built in the 1550s, amidst the 125-acre walled vineyard of Clos de Vougeot. Forbidding as it looks, it repays a visit. There are guided tours throughout the day (11.30am–2.00pm excluded) which include the *Grand Cellier* in which the château's owners,

the *Confrérie des Chevaliers du Tastevin*, hold their frequent indulgent feasts and ceremonies.
*21640 Vougeot. Tel (80) 06–86–09*

### CHÂTEAU CORTON-ANDRÉ

The gorgeous gilded mosaic roof of this immaculate castle (it dates back to the 1400s) is the unmistakable landmark of Aloxe-Corton, the tiny hamlet at the foot of the famed hill of Corton. The château is the headquarters of the distinguished wine firm Pierre André – all of whose wines are labelled with the image of the celebrated roof. You can taste and buy the firm's wines here.
*21920 Aloxe-Corton.*
*Tel (80) 26–44–25.*
*Open daily 10am–6pm*

### MUSÉE DU VIN DE BOURGOGNE

In the old centre of Beaune, housed in the 15th-century Logis du Roi – once the seat of

*The famous walled vineyard of Le Montrachet to the west of Puligny-Montrachet*

*A distant view of the village of Pommard with the vine covered hillsides of the Côte de Beaune rising up behind*

the dukes of Burgundy – this splendid museum displays a rich collection of fine art as well as the historic impedimenta of wine. Included is a well-illustrated exhibition of how Burgundy winemaking from vineyard to bottle has evolved over the centuries.
*Logis du Roi, 21200 Beaune.*
*Tel (80) 22–08–19.*
Open daily 9–11.30am and 2–5.30pm.

## HÔTEL DIEU

Beaune's most famous building is the extravagant hospital purpose-built in the 1400s at the behest of the charitable Chancellor of Burgundy (it was then a sovereign duchy) Nicholas Rolin and his wife, Guigone de Salins. A Flemish fantasy of gables and galleries, turrets and finials, all under an extraordinary mosaic roof that would do credit to a tropical butterfly, this is one of the great buildings of France. Known locally as the Hospices de

Beaune, it is now a museum (a new hospital, immediately behind, fulfils its former role), and, most famously, the venue for the annual auction of wines from estates owned by the Hospices, which takes places in November. This event is ticket-only, but do visit the museum, which has a gorgeous collection of tapestries and much other fine art.
*Place de la Halle, 21200 Beaune.*
*(Tel (80) 22–24–51).*
*Enquire at the Tourist Information office opposite the Hôtel Dieu about opening times*

## PATRIARCHE PÈRE & FILS

Of numerous companies with extensive cellars in Beaune, Patriarche is probably the largest, and is well organised to cope with visitors. Founded in the 1780s the firm bought the splendid convent of the Nuns of the Visitation in Beaune in the sell-off of ecclesiastical possessions during the French

Revolution, and in the endless cellars below it now lie millions of bottles of Patriarche wine. Included is the company's best-known mass-market product, Kriter sparkling wine. Many fine burgundies are also available for tasting. There are regular tours, and the modest fee is paid to charity.
*Ancien Couvent des Visitandines,*
*Rue Paul Chanson, 21204 Beaune.*
*Tel (80) 22–23–20.*

## LA REINE PÉDAUQUE

Another large firm with cellars to visit, this time at the former Relais des Diligences (the

which takes in the vast modern *chais* (ground-level cellar) complete with Gallo-Roman-style vaulting, all built in pre-cast concrete in 1984.
*Les Vignes de la Croix, BP 06, 71390 Buxy.*
*Tel (85) 92–03–03.*

## MAISON DES VINS DE LA CÔTE CHALONNAISE

For information on all varieties of Chalonnais wines and about the different growers. A good range of the wines is available here for tasting.
*Promenade Ste Marie, 71000 Chalon-sur-Saône.*
*Tel (85) 41–64–00.*

## ANTONIN RODET

One of the great Burgundy firms, based at Mercurey, Rodet has interests throughout the region which include two beautiful Chalonnais châteaux, at Chamirey and Rully, the estates of which produce outstanding wines. The firm's '*Maison de reception*' is well worth a visit.
*Mercurey, 71640 Givry.*
*Tel (85) 45–22–22.*
Open 9am–12.30pm and 1.30–6pm, Mon to Fri.

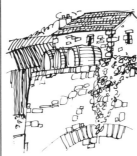

## MAISON MÂCONNAISE DES VINS

Visit for information on the wines and the growers. There is a wide range of Mâconnais wines on sale and even a restaurant serving fairly priced, simple local dishes.
*Avenue de Lattre-de-Tassigny, 71000 Mâcon. Tel (85) 38–36–70.*

grandest hotel in Beaune during the last century) at one of the town's impressive gates, the Porte St Nicholas. More than 200,000 people come to taste and buy at this fascinating 'exhibition cellar' every year. By Beaune standards, the prices are quite reasonable for the undoubtedly high quality that some of the wines are.
*Caves-Exposition de la Reine Pédauque, Porte St Nicholas, 21200 Beaune.*
*Tel (80) 22–23–11.*

## CHALONNAIS & MACONNAIS

### CAVES DES VIGNERONS DE BUXY

Big modern co-operative doing a roaring trade in *vente directe* of excellent Chalonnais wines – half their sales are to visitors loading a crate or two into the family saloon. Innovative winemaking techniques can be seen in action here on a tour,

## BEAUJOLAIS

### LA MAISON DES BEAUJOLAIS

The information centre for wine tours of the region, and also a rather good restaurant serving local specialities.
*On the N6, 69220 St Jean d'Ardières. Tel (74) 66–16–46.*

## MOULIN À VENT

Of the ten *Crus* of Beaujolais – the individual parishes making wines they can label with their own names rather than as simple Beaujolais-Villages – Moulin à Vent is regarded as the most 'serious', a wine to keep a few years before drinking. You can taste the wine right next to the 17th-century sailless windmill from which it takes its name, in the Caveau du Moulin à Vent. Note that, curiously, there is no village of the name – the windmill stands just north of Romanèche-Thorins.
*Romanèche-Thorins, 71570 La Chapelle de Guinchay.*
*Caveau closed Tuesday.*

## JULIÉNAS

Another *Cru*, this time named after the village where, reputedly, the first Beaujolais grapes were planted in the time of Julius (thus Juliénas) Caesar. Like all the *Crus*, it has its own *caveau de dégustation*, with the distinction that this one is in a redundant church. 'It is worth bearing in mind,' one travel writer warns, 'that the murals with which it is now decorated are extremely uninhibited'.
*Le Cellier de la Vieille Église, 69840 Juliénas.*

# Gastronomic Specialities

*Beaune's bustling Saturday market*

**À LA BOURGUIGNONNE** signifies a dish cooked not simply in the wine of the region, but in the generous, homely style that typifies Burgundian cuisine. Take a classic recipe for four servings of **BŒUF BOURGUIGNON**. The marinade alone calls for a whole bottle of red burgundy. Locally, the stew is made with the lean and rather chewy meat of the Charolais – the cream-coloured cattle that seem to crowd every Burgundy pasture. Up to four hours' simmering is called for in a rich sauce of wine, onions, carrots, garlic, herbs and spices, plus a garnish of bacon, shallots and mushrooms.

**COQ AU VIN** rivals the beef stew for renown – and for the labour-intensiveness demanded by its recipes. The origin of the dish is in its ability to make the most of a tough old cock bird, first by marinating it in wine, then sautéeing, and finally cooking it in a delectable sauce of wine, vegetables and herbs for up to two hours.

**POULARDE** is the name given to the plump young chickens of Bresse, across the River Saône from Beaujolais, and said to be the finest poultry in France. The chickens must be raised free-range and corn-fed (witness the huge fields of maize in the region) to be sold with the Bresse name. In the markets of Beaune, Dijon or Mâcon, you can recognise Bresse birds by their blue feet – and high price. Tender and flavoursome, these chickens are at their best simply roasted. On menus, look out for **POULARDE DE BRESSE RÔTIE** or **POULARDE EN DEMI-DEUIL** ('chicken in half-mourning', so known because slices of black Burgundian truffles are threaded into the white meat of the bird).

**CHARCUTERIE** In Lyon, at Burgundy's southern end, they take their *saucissons* seriously. The city's company of *charcutiers* was formed in 1543, and remains very much in business. From Lyon itself comes the famed **ROSETTE**, a salami-like pork sausage which has a delicious spicy version with the same name in the Chalonnais district, made with the addition of red

**ESCARGOTS À LA BOURGUIGNONNE** Burgundy's snails grow fat among the vines, only to end up cooked in the white wine, and served in the traditional manner with butter and garlic, shallots and parsley. The restaurants of Mâcon make a particular speciality of this celebrated starter, offering 6, 9 or even 12 snails a serving – the latter quantity defying all but the most heroic appetites.

**POCHOUSE** is a traditional stew of freshwater fish from the region's great rivers, the Saône and Rhône. Carp, perch, pike, salmon and trout are customary ingredients, as is eel to give richness. Bacon adds flavour and the sauce, which should include some dry white burgundy, is enriched with butter and cream. In the Mâconnais, this dish takes the name **MATELOTE** – and employs red Mâcon wine instead of white.

**QUENELLES DE BROCHET** is another classic fish dish of the region. *Quenelles* are in effect small sausages, made from pulped pike (*brochet*). A sauce of *écrevisses* (crayfish, also from the local rivers) usually accompanies the dish.

**MOUTARDE** Dijon is the unchallenged capital of the mustard world, claiming even to have given the great condiment its name – from the motto on the town's heraldic arms, granted in 1382, *Moult Me Tarde* (meaning 'much awaits me'). The description *à la dijonnais* has thus come to identify any Burgundian recipe flavoured with mustard.

**CÔTES DE VEAU DIJONNAISE** – veal chops with mustard – is a classic, in which the chops are browned, then simmered in wine, stock and herbs. Cream is added once the meat is cooked, and the mustard stirred in at the last minute; the mustard is never boiled as this would turn it bitter.

**OEUFS BRESSANE** is among a myriad chocolate-based delights relished from Lyon northwards – blown eggs are filled with *ganache* (chocolate, double cream and Grand Marnier) and *praline* (almonds and sugar).

**Fromage Frais** Burgundians like to eat their cheeses fresh, when still creamy, and ideally with a dollop of fresh cream and a little sugar – just like a pudding. Mature cheeses of the region include **ÉPOISSES**, a cylindrical cow's milk variety with the brick-coloured rind that results from washings with the local spirit, *marc de Bourgogne*. Reputedly Napoleon's favourite cheese, it has a soft texture and very tangy flavour. **ST FLORENTIN**, **CITEAUX** and **SOUMAINTRAIN** are similar, but are all disc-shaped and with paler rinds. **BOUTON DE CULOTTE** is a tiny cylinder of *chèvre* (goat's cheese) with a firm texture and, when newly made, a rich and deliciously pungent flavour. The name means 'trouser-button' and the cheese comes from Mâcon – just one of a score of goat's cheeses from Burgundy that are rarely found outside the region.

peppers. In the Beaujolais, **JAMBON PERSILLÉ** is a delectable dome of local Morvan ham cooked in white wine and layered slice after slice with chopped parsley.

**ANDOUILLETTES DE CHABLIS** are the famous wine town's delicious rendering of the classic tripe sausage of the region – best eaten freshly scorched from the frying pan and washed down with an ice-cold draught of Chablis *Premier Cru*.

**OEUFS À LA BOURGUIGNONNE** are eggs poached in red burgundy and served on *croûtons*. A variation is to mix the poaching wine with sauce or stock – one recipe is **OEUFS POCHÉS EN MEURETTE**, which comes with a garnish of bacon, mushrooms and sautéed baby onions. The result is delicious, but very rich.

# Hotels and Restaurants

*A village house with its cellar in the Beaujolais village of Montmelas*

## CHABLIS-YONNE

### HOSTELLERIE DES CLOS

Smartish new hotel in the converted buildings of the ancient Clos des Hospices in Chablis. The 26 rooms have simple comforts, but the plush modern restaurant aspires to great things – it has one Michelin star already. Proprietor-chef Michel Vigneau's specialities include wonderful fish dishes (try the *suprême de sandre à l'Irancy*, based on young pike) with which to quaff the local wines. Closed Jan. Restaurant closed Wed, and Thur lunch, Oct 1 to May 31.
*Rue Jules Rathier, 89800 Chablis.*
*Tel (86) 42–10–63.*

### AUBERGE DU BIEF

*Pochouse*, the famed Burgundian freshwater-fish stew, is among the delicious traditional dishes to try from the fairly priced menu of this popular local restaurant, 'five minutes from Chablis, out of the hustle and bustle and in a floral decor' as owner Serge Baffet puts it. Closed first two weeks of Oct, and Mon evening and Tues out of season.
*2 Avenue de Chablis, 89144 Ligny le Châtel.*
*Tel (86) 47–43–42.*

### LE SAINT BRIS

Cheerful bistro with authentically faded posters lining its smoke-blackened walls; cooking according to what is in season, with mouthwatering *plats du jour* chalked up on a blackboard. The *escargots en croûte* are superb, and the green salads, dressed with walnut oil, are inspirational. It is on the corner facing the medieval centre of St Bris, and well worth seeking out. Just 70FF for the set menu. Closed Mon evenings and Tue.
*89530 St Bris le Vineux.*
*Tel (86) 53–84–56.*

### L'ABBAYE ST MICHEL

At Tonnerre, 10 miles east of Chablis along the D 965, this chic and expensive restaurant-with-rooms has every comfort within its walls – with beautiful gardens and tennis court beyond. Two stars in Michelin. Closed Jan 1 to mid-Feb. Restaurant closed Tues lunch and Thur Oct to Apr.
*Rue St Michel, Tonnerre, 89700 Yonne.*
*Tel (86) 55–05–99.*

## COTE D'OR

### CHEZ JEANNETTE

At Fixin, northernmost of the Côte d'Or *Appellation Contrôlée* districts, just 7 miles south of Dijon, a simple village inn with a good restaurant and very reasonable prices. Closed Christmas to end Jan. Restaurant closed Thur.
*7 Rue Noisot, Fixin, 21200 Gevrey-Chambertin.*
*Tel (80) 52–45–49.*

### LES MILLESIMES

A small and highly rated restaurant in a converted 18th-century cellar at Gevrey-Chambertin. Specialities include *gratin de queues d'écrevisses* (crayfish in a rich cream sauce with cheese) and *pigeonneau aux echalotes confites* (pigeon with pickled onions) and the *carte des vins* runs to 1,350 different wines. Prices are surprisingly good. Closed Jan to early Feb, Tue and Wed lunch.
*25 Rue de L'Eglise, Gevrey-Chambertin, 21220 Côte d'Or.*
*Tel (8) 51–84–24.*

### CÔTE D'OR

The locals whisper reverential praise of this Michelin two-star restaurant in Nuits-St-Georges. Try the sublime variation on the snail theme, *escargots de Bourgogne en cocotte lutée*. There are seven comfortable bedrooms. Exclusive and expensive. Closed Feb and on Sun evenings and Wed.
*37 Rue Thurot, 21700 Nuits-St-Georges.*
*Tel (80) 61–06–10.*

### HOTEL CLARION

Small but smart hotel in the village of Aloxe-Corton, idyllically set at the foot of the hill of Corton. Much *art nouveau* decor. Closed Jan.
*21420 Aloxe-Corton.*
*Tel (80) 26–46–70.*

### HOTEL DE LA POSTE

Well-regarded hotel with 25 rooms on the busy Beaune bypass (so try to get a room facing out to the rear). Very good restaurant with many fish specialities and a lavish wine list. The hotel is particularly popular with American visitors, and the service is outstanding. Expensive. Closed Nov 21 to Mar 24.
*1 Boulevard Clémenceau, 21200 Beaune.*
*Tel (80) 22–08–11.*

*A cottage in the village of Sampigny-les-Maranges in the southern region of the Côte de Beaune*

### LA CLOSERIE

30-room hotel, without a restaurant, just south of Beaune. Comfortable and economical, just the place to explore the region from – which is what its many wine-merchant customers use it for. Closed Christmas to end Jan.
*61 Route de Pommard, 21200 Beaune. Tel (80) 22–15–07.*

### LE CEP

An adapted 17th-century townhouse, furnished in keeping with its period, this elegant hotel in the centre of Beaune has every luxury but one – a dining room. The restaurant next door, the Bernard Morillon, fills the gap admirably. Hotel closed Dec to end Feb. Restaurant closed Feb, and Tue and Wed lunch from Nov 20 to end Mar.

*27 Rue Maufoux, 21200 Beaune. Tel (80) 22–35–48.*

### LE RELAIS DE SAULX

Monsieur Monnoir's small and friendly restaurant offers *haute cuisine* at prices that attract much local custom – so you must book in advance to be sure of a table. Bresse chicken dishes are always excellent and there is a formidable *chariot de desserts*. Closed third week in Jun, first

week in Sep; mid-Feb to Mid-Mar closed Sun evenings and Mon.
*6 Rue Louis-Véry, 21200 Beaune. Tel (80) 22–01–35.*

### LE RELAIS DE LA DILIGENCE

Near the station at Meursault, just south of the village itself, a simple restaurant serving traditional Burgundian dishes – including wonderful *coq au vin* – at positively rustic prices. Closed mid-Dec to early Feb, and Tue evening and Wed.
*À la Gare, 21190 Meursault. Tel (80) 21–21–32.*

### LE MONTRACHET

Unpretentious hotel overlooking the village green at Puligny-Montrachet. The quiet restaurant is an absolute treat, offering speciality dishes

restaurant with three Michelin stars. In what was once a very grand house dating from the 15th century, master chef Jacques Lameloise and his wife have created a lavish 20-room hotel and outstanding restaurant. Dishes are faithful to the region, the chocolate desserts are legendary, the wine list comprehensive – and the prices appropriate. Closed from third week in Dec to mid-Jan, and Wed and Thur lunch.
*Place d'Armes, 71150 Chagny.*
*Tel (85) 87–08–85.*

### HOTEL LE COMMERCE

Simple, 16-room inn at Rully, with a comfortable dining-room serving delicious local dishes at affordable prices. Closed Mon.
*Place Ste Marie, 71150 Rully.*
*Tel (85) 87–20–09.*

### HOSTELLERIE DU VAL D'OR

Top-flight restaurant with a notable list of Chalonnaiş wines and very attractive prices. There are 11 comfortable bedrooms. Owner Jean-Claude Cogny's enthusiasm for Burgundian cuisine is charming and infectious. Closed at several times of year, so check in advance.
*On the D 978 at Mercurey, 71640 Givry.*
*Tel (85) 45–13–70.*

### FRANTEL

In the town centre at Mâcon, overlooking the river, a modern 60-room hotel with a surprisingly good restaurant serving local specialities rather than the 'international cuisine' you might expect! Closed Sat lunch.
*26 Rue de Coubertin, 71000 Mâcon.*
*Tel (85) 38–28–02.*

### RELAIS DE SOLUTRÉ

With views over the vineyards of Pouilly-Fuissé, and the vast rock of Solutré, a 25-room hotel with an interesting restaurant

arranged round a large woodburning stove. Comfortable and informal – and good value. Closed Jan to mid-Feb and on Mon.
*Solutré-Pouilly 71960.*
*Tel (85) 35–80–81.*

### CHATEAU DE PIZAY

Grand hotel in a quaintly turreted castle dating from the 14th century, near the Beaujolais *Grand Cru* village of Morgon. Good restaurant with set menus at attractive prices. The *fillet de bœuf clouté* is delicious. Open all year.
*Saint Jean d'Ardières, 69220 Belleville sur Saône.*
*Tel (74) 66–51–41.*

### COQ AU VIN

No prizes for guessing the speciality of this charming little restaurant-with-rooms in the village of Juliénas. Delicious, simple food, and plenty of it. Closed Dec to end Feb, and on Wed.
*Place du Marché, 69840 Juliénas.*
*Tel (74) 04–41–98.*

### AUBERGE DU CEP

Fashionable (two stars in Michelin) restaurant in the most fashionable of the Beaujolais villages, Fleurie. The cooking is inspired, the choice of Fleurie wines excellent, and the prices rather high. Closed early Aug and for Christmas and New Year holidays, and Sun evenings and Thur.
*Place de l'Eglise, 69820 Fleurie.*
*Tel (74) 04–10–77.*

including *Blanc de volaille de Bresse au foie gras*, and an exceptional range of local cheeses. Prices are very fair for the rather motel-like rooms, and even better for the menus. A ten-minute stroll from this hotel takes you into the famous vineyards of Puligny-Montrachet, and to that of the great Le Montrachet itself. Closed Dec to Mid-Jan; restaurant closed Wed.
*21190 Puligny-Montrachet.*
*Tel (80) 21–30–06.*

### CHALONNAIS & MACONNAIS

### HOTEL LAMELOISE

Chagny, which has the distinction of being twinned with Letchworth in Hertfordshire, has the further *cachet* of possessing Burgundy's only

# Calendar of Events

### JANUARY

22nd – Festival of St Vincent in Champlitte (Haute-Saône)

Sunday nearest 22nd – Festival of St Vincent in Gevrey-Chambertin (Côte d'Or)

Sunday nearest 22nd – Wine show in Château d'Aine Aze (Saône-et-Loire)

Sunday nearest 22nd – Wine show in Mâcon (Saône-et-Loire)

*A winter scene in the vineyards of Pommard in the Côte de Beaune*

Sunday nearest 22nd – Festival of St Vincent in Coulanges-la-Vineuse (Yonne)

### MARCH

Saturday before Palm Sunday – Wine fair in Lugny (Saône-et-Loire)

### APRIL

End of the month – Wine auction in Nuits-St-George (Côte d'Or)

### END APRIL/ BEGINNING MAY

Election of queen of the wines of the Mâconnais in Château d'Aine (Saône-et-Loire)

## MAY

3rd week – Mâcon fair and French wines competition in Mâcon (Saône-et-Loire)

## JULY

3rd Sunday – Wine festival in Arbois (Jura)

## AUGUST

15th – Vin de Table fair in Chagny (Saône-et-Loire)

Last weekend – Wine festival in St Pourcin-sur-Sioule/Allier (Auvergne)

## SEPTEMBER

Savoie fair in Chambéry (Savoie)

1st Sunday – Fêtes de Biou wine festival in Arbois (Jura)

9th/10th – International festival of wines in Dijon (Côte d'Or)

Middle of the month – Wine festival in St Jean-de-Vaux (Saône-et-Loire)

## OCTOBER

Last Saturday – Fête Raclet, exhibition and sale of Beaujolais Primeur in Romanèche-Thorins (Saône-et-Loire)

End of the month – Presentation of Beaujolais Primeurs in Lacenas (Rhône)

## NOVEMBER

Beginning of the month – Sale and exhibition of Beaujolais Crus in Fleurie (Rhône)

1st fortnight – Gastronomic fair in Dijon (Côte d'Or)

2nd weekend – Sauvignon festival in St Bris-le-Vineux (Yonne)

Middle of the month – Exhibition and competition of Crus Juliénas in Juliénas (Rhône)

End of the month – Exhibition and competition of Brouilly and Côtes de Brouilly in Cercie (Rhône)

3rd weekend – *Les Trois Glorieuses* wine fair of the Côte d'Or in Beaune.
Saturday: Château Clos de Vougeot; Sunday: auction in the market then dinner in the Hospices de Beaune; Monday: Paulée de Meursault

Last Saturday – Wine fair in Chablis (Yonne)

## DECEMBER

1st weekend – Competition and exhibition of the 11 Crus Appellations of Beaujolais in Villefranche (Rhône)

Middle of the month – Baptême Parisien of the Beaujolais Nouveau in Villefranche (Rhône)

Middle of the month – Sale of the Hospice de Beaujeu wines in Beaujeu (Rhône)

# Index